I0120946

Putnam County Tennessee

Diaries, Letters, Wills

and

Other Records

WPA RECORDS

Heritage Books
2024

HERITAGE BOOKS

AN IMPRINT OF HERITAGE BOOKS, INC.

Books, CDs, and more—Worldwide

For our listing of thousands of titles see our website
at
www.HeritageBooks.com

A Facsimile Reprint
Published 2024 by
HERITAGE BOOKS, INC.
Publishing Division
5810 Ruatan Street
Berwyn Heights, MD 20740

Originally published 1936

— Publisher's Notice —
In reprints such as this, it is often not possible to remove
blemishes from the original. We feel the contents of this
book warrant its reissue despite these blemishes and
hope you will agree and read it with pleasure.

International Standard Book Number
Paperbound: 978-0-7884-8989-1

WPA RECORDS

The WPA Records are, for the most part, carbon copies of the original that was typed on onion skin paper during the Depression. Since these records were typed on poor machines by people who did not type well either and read by persons not always sure of the older handwritten material, the results are often less that perfect.

We have made every attempt to make as good a copy as can be made from these older papers. Sometimes there are water stains and burned edges around the paper.. This is the results of a fire at the home of one of the workers, Mrs. Penelope Allen, who was over most of the project.

The WPA Records are now very scattered between the State Archives, various Public and Private Libraries and other collections. Some day, there is a hope that all of these can be collected and stored in one place. In spite of their many mistakes and problems, these are still the most complete collection of Tennessee records found anywhere.

TENNESSEE

RECORDS OF PUTNAM COUNTY

MISCELLANEOUS RECORDS
(DIARIES, LETTERS, WILLS, INDENTURES, ETC.)

COPIED UNDER WORKS PROGRESS ADMINISTRATION

HISTORICAL RECORDS PROJECT
Official Project No. 65-44-1487

MRS. JOHN TROTWOOD MORE
STATE LIBRARIAN & ARCHIVIST, SPONSOR

MRS. ELIZABETH D. COPPEDGE
STATE DIRECTOR OF WOMEN'S & PROFESSIONAL PROJECTS

MRS. PENELOPE JOHNSON ALLEN
STATE SUPERVISOR

MRS. RHEA E. GARRETT
MISS MATILDA A. PORTER
DISTRICT SUPERVISORS

COPYISTS

MISS PEARL KUYKENDALL
MRS. ALLIE LOFTIS
MRS. JOHN RICHARDSON

AUGUST 1936

MISCELLANEOUS RECORDS
DIARIES, LETTERS, WILLS, INDENTURES, ETC.

INDEX

A

B

Byers, 52
Byrne, 82,138
Byrne, Ann, 131,139
Byrne, Brice, 139,140,141
Byrne, Dallas, 86
Byrne, L., (Esq.) 139

C

Cadmus, 47
Cage, John, 2,3
Cain, John, 36
Cahahan, W. M., 16
Calhan, W. W., 14
Camard, W., 86
Cameron, A., 86
Cameron, Mo., 89
Cameron, S., 86
Cameron, S. O., 86
Camp Chattanooga, 145
Camp Trousdale, 142,143
Campbell, 53
Camson,, S., 86
Cane Creek, 53,54,56,79
Caney Fork, 29,31,47,60,82,99,129,
  136
Cannon County, 103,115
Cannon, N., 69,91
Cannon, N. (Gov.) 54
Cannon, Newton, 61,69,91
Cannon, Newton (Gov.) 54
Caplinger, Samuel, 11
Capner, Samuel, 15
Car, Elijah, 96,97
Carden (Lieut Col.) 103
Carland, J., 85,400
Carland, James, 85
Carlen, J., 85
Carlinger, Samuel, 6
Carlisle, Simon, 58,59,61
Carlton, John M., 101
Carnes, Beeton, 104
Carr, C., 13
Carr, Henry, 55,77
Carr, James, 55
Carr, W. H., 94
Carr, William, 95
Carroll (Gov.) 88
Carroll, William, 67,72,78,88,91,
  92,94
Carroll, William (Gov.) 28,40,41,
  44,68
Carroll, Wm., 28,73,78,92,94,95
Carroll, Wm. (Gov.) 30,41,44,87,
  129
Carson, George, 79,80
Carson, James, 80

Carson,Nathan, 80
Carsons, Nehemiah, 79,80
Carter, F., 96
Carter, F. C., 96
Carter, Sion, 96
Carthage, 47
Cass, Lew, 66
Cassetty, S. W., 101
Cassetty, Sampson W., 101
Cates, Thomas, 101
Cath, Mary, 122
Crowell Catholic Cathedral, 49
Carve, C., 17
Cedar Bridge, 37
Cedar Creek, 12,15,24
Chaffin, 107
Chanard, W., 86
Charley, 125
Chattanooga, 105,106,107,110
Chesapeake Bay, 109,112
Cheatham County, 103
Chestnut Mound, 72
Chestnut Mound, Tenn., 58
Chicamauga River, 106
Chind (negro) 98
Choat, John, 57
Choate, Thomas, 92,94,95,97
Claborn, W., 122
Claiborn, A., 122
Claiborn, Amelia Weldon, 118
Claiborn, Bettie, 127
Clark, 3,18,136
Clark, Benjamin, 1,3,6,18
Clark, Gilbert, 1
Clark, Henry B., 70
Clark, Isaac, 88,96
Clark, J. D., 65
Claysville, 84
Cleburne's Brigade, 10
Cleghorn, John, 43
Clement, Ann H. (Mrs.) 126
City Point, 109,112
Cobey, Fern, 85
Cofeld, Willis, 12
Cofell, Willie, 10
Cofell, Willis, 9,10
Coffee County, 103
Coffeld, Willis, 12
Cole, Anderson, 98
Cole, Josiah, 32
Coleman, Jim, 110
College Grove, 106
Collins, 91
Collins, William, 76,77
Columbia, Tenn. 118
Confederate Army, 111
Cook, C. W., 51
Choat, Austin, 98

G

1

PUTNAM COUNTY

FAMILY RECORD
JAMES PRIM - WILLIAM ALGOOD MONTGOMERY DEED
1808

Owned by Mrs. Lula Algood and Mrs. Alfred Algood, Cookeville, Tennessee.

Copied by Miss Pearl Kuykendall, Mrs. Allie Loftis, Mrs. John Richardson.

This indenture made this eleventh day of July in the Year of our Lord
One thousand Eight hundred and Eight Between James Prim of the County of
Wilson and State of Tennessee of the one part and William Algood
Montgomery County and State of North Carolina of the other part witnesseth that the said James Prim for and in consideration of the sum of Two
hundred and Thirty five Dollars te him in hand paid on or before the Sealing
or delivering of these presents the receipt of is hereby acknowledged by the
aforesaid James Prim unto the aforesaid William Algood and the said James
Prim for himself his heirs doth hereby bargain sale and convey and confirm
unto him the aforesaid William Algood his Heirs Executors Administrators
and assigns forever a certain tract or parcel of Land situated in Wilson
County and State of aforesaid and bounded as follows viz: Beginning on a poplar at the South west corner of the field in Benjamin Clarks line and running from said poplar North Seventeen degrees West twelve poles to a Hickory
& whit Oak Thence North Seventy degrees west forty poles to a small Hickory
on the top of a ridge thence North sixty five poles to a dogwood thence
East forty two poles to a dogwood thence North Twenty four poles to a beach
thence East fifty Two poles to a stake thence South one hundred and eighty
poles to a stake said Prims Corner thence West to the beginning by estimation fifty five acres and one half including the plantation whereon Thomas
McClendon now lives be the same more or less which trade or parcel of Land
with all and every of its appurtenances thereunto belonging or otherwise
appertaining the said James Prim for himself his heirs Executors Administrators or assigns hath hereby sold Conveyed Released and confirmed unto
the said William Algood his heirs Executors Administreators and assigns
and the said James Prim for himself his heirs to and with the said William
Algood his heirs & that the said James Prim his heirs & shall warrent and
forever defend the same Land with all and every of its members from all
Lawful claims or Claim of any Person or persons unto the said William
Algood and his heirs assigns forever in witness whereof I have hereunto
set my hand and Seal the day and year above wirtten in presents of John M
Gee

James Prim (X) his mark   SEAL

Elmore Douglas Ackd.
Gilbert Clark
State of Tennessee Wilson County I, Henry Ross Register of said County I
do hereby certify that the written Deed is duly Registered in Book D. P,
298 the 25th February 1811.

Henry Ross Register

James Prim 55½ acres
      Deed to
William Algood
Recorded in Book D. Page 198

This Indenture made this fourth day of December in the Year of Our Lord onr Thousand Eight hundred and Eleven Between John Cage of the County of Wilson and State of Tennessee of the one part and William Algood of the County and State aforesaid of the other part Witnesseth that the said John Cage for and in the consideration of the sum of five hundred Dollars to him in Hand paid the Receipt whereof is hereby acknowledged hath bargained Sold conveyed and confirmed unto the aforesaid William Algood a certain trad or parcel of Land lying in the County of Wilson and Tennessee near the Cumberland River and bounded as follows Beginning on McDowells South Boundry line of a six Hindred andforty one acre Tract on an E——— and running South one hundred and eighty four poles to as ash and hickory thence East one Hundred and Eighty poles to an Hickory thence North two Hundred and twenty eight poles to a white oak Thence West one hundred & fifty six poles to a Hickory on McDanials East boundry line thence South with said line forty four poles to said McDanials corner thence poles to the Beginning and Joining Twenty five Acres be the same more or less which said tract or parcel of Land with all and every appurtenances thereunto belonging to said John Cage for himself his Heirs Executers Administrators or assigns hath hereby sold delivered conveyed and confirmed to the said William Algood his heirs executors Administrators or assignsand said John Cage doth for himself his heirs Executers and Administraters hereby covenant with the said William Algood his Heirs Executers Administrators or as assigns that the said John Cage his Heirs Executers Administrators will wax rent emebers and appurtenances thereunto belonging free from all claims of any person or Persons whatsoever unto the said William Algood his heirs Executors Administrators or assigns forever In witness whereof the said John Cage hath set his Hand and affixed heis seal the day and Date above written Signed Sealed and Delivered in the Presence of Wirt Jones Jared John Jared

Douglas Jared (SEAL)

State of Tennesse Wilson County
    Of said County certificate Duly Registered
13- 1813

RECORDS OF MRS. LULA ALGOOD (CON)

This Indenture made this fourth Day fo November in the Year of Four Lord one Thousand Eight hundred and Twelve between Benjamin Clark andthe County of Wilson and State of Tennessee one part and William Algood of h the county and State aforesaid of the other part. Witness that the said Benjamin Clark for and in the consideration of the sum of five Hundred and Eight Dollars him in Hand paid the Receipt whereof is hereby acknowl- edged hath bargained sold conveyed and confirmed unto the aforesaid Wil- liam Algood a ceratin Tract or parcel of Land Lying in the County of Wil- son State of Tennessee and Bpunded as follows on a Whiye oak in the Road leading from Said Clarks to the place where John Cage formerly Resided Be- longing to William Algood and Running South thirtytwo degrees West fifty nine Poles to a post oak and Hickory in Hambletons line Thence East twenty twe Poles to a Hickory and black oak said Clarks North west corner of a hun- dred Acres purchased of Hambletons Thence South one hundred and Clarks North West corner of a hundred Acres fiekd East one hundred and forty poke to an ash and fourteen poles to a Hickory and Sugar tree thence to a black oak said Hambletons North East Corner of a six hundred and forty poles/ Acre T act thence West fouteen Poles to a Hickory and Dogwood thence North fifty nine Poles to a Spanish oak and two Ironwoods on Elmore Douglas line thenceWest three Degrees South one Hundred and twenty six poles to the beginning- Including one Hundred and forty Acres of Land be the same more or less, which said traector parcel of Land with all and every appertenanceh thereunto belonging the said Banjamming Clark for himself his Heirs Ex- ecutors Administrators and Assigns hath hereby Sold delivered conveyed and confirmed the William Algood administrators and assigns hathhereby Sold del- livered the said Benjamin Clark deth for himself his heirs there administra- tors Executors or assigns hereby covenant with the said William A;good his heirs Executors Administrators and assigns that the said Benjamin Clark his Heirs Executers Administraters and Assigns Shall and willwarrent and defend forever the said trade or parcel of Land with all and every of its members and Appertenances thereunto belong free from Claims of any Person or Person whatsoever unto the said William Algood his Heirs Executors Administrators or Assigns for ever In witness whereof the said Benjamin Clark hath set his Hand and Affixed his S al the day and Date Above written Signed S_ealed and Delivered in the Presance of

Reech A. Holdman
Wm Bable
John Botuma
Benjamin Clark SEAL
Ackd

State of Tennessee Wilson County March Term 1813
    The within deed of bargain and Sale from Benjamin Clark to William Algd for 140 acres of land was duly acknowl edged in open court by said Clark ordered to be Registered
            Test- John Allcorn   Clerkof Wilson County
State of Tennessee Wilson County Registers office Aprile lo, 1813
I, Henry Ross Register of Wilson Countydo hereby certify thatthe forsgoing deed is certificate are duly registered in Book E. Page 138
            Test- Henry Ross Registered of Wilsoh County
Benjamin Clark to Deed William Algood
Registered in Book E. Page 138 Deed 14 acres

This Indenture made this fifteenth Day of June in the Year of Our Lord
one Thousand Eight hundred and Fourteen between Elmore Douglas of the
County of Smith and State of Tennessee of the one part and William Algood
of the County Wilson and State of Tennessee of the other part Witnesseth that
the Said Elmore Douglas for and in the Consideration of the Sum of fifty
Dollars to him in hand paid the receipt where of is hereby acknowledged hath
bargained Sold conveyed and Confirmed unto the afore said William Algood a
certain Tract or parcel of Land lying in the County of Wilson and State of
Tennessee and Bounded as follows beginning on a sugar Tree Hardy Hunters
corner in Elmore Douglas West boundry line and Running South between eighty
and one hundred Poles to a Stake nine poles and three Quarters North of he
spring thence West to a Stake thence North to Hardy Hunters line thence
East to the beginning including Eight acres and sixty four poles of Land
be the same more or less which said Tract or parcel of Land with all and
veery appertinence thereunto belonging to the said Elmore Douglas for himself his heirs Executors Administrators or Assigns hath hereby Sold delivered conveyed and confirmed to the said William Algood his heirs Executors
Administrators or assigns hereby covenant with the said William Algood his
heirs Exors Administrators or assigns that the said Elmore Douglasm his,
heirs & C shall and will warrant and defenf forever the said Tract or parcl
of Land with all and every of to numbers and appertenences from all claim
of any person or persons whtso ever unto the said William Algood his Heirs
& C forever ,

In witness whereof the said Elmore Douglas hath set his Handn and affixed his seal the Day and Date above written
Signed and Sealed and De ivered in the Presance

                                              Elmore Douglas   (SEAL)
                                                   Asked.

State of Tennessee Wilson County Court June Term 1814, Thw within Deed of
barganer and Sale from Elmore Douglas to William Algood was duly acknowledge
in the open court by the bargainer and ordered to be Registered
                         Attest—John Allcorn Clerk of Wilson County
State of Tennessee Wilson County Registers office the 5th of August 1814
The Weather deed of a bargnin and Sale and clerk certificate thereon are
duly Registered in Book E. Page 341
                         Attest—Henry Ross Register of Wilson County

Deed   8-64poles
Elmore Douglas
   To William Algood 107
Registered in Book E. Page 341

RECORDS OWNED BY MRS. ALFRED ALGOOD, COOKEVILLE, TENN

This Indenture made this twenty fourth of December in the year of Our Lord one thousand eight hundred and fiveteen between Elmore Douglas of the county of Smith and State of Tennessee of the one part and William Algood of the County of Wilson State of Tennessee of the other part. Witness that the said Elmore Douglas and in the consideration of the sum of Fifty Dollars to him in Hand paid the receipt whereof is hereby acknowledged that bargainedshould conveyed and confirmed unto the said William Algood a certin tracet or parcel of Land lying in the County of Wilson and State of Tennesseeand bounded as follows: beginning at the SouthEast Corner of a fifty five and one half acre Tract Deeded to said Algood by Kames Prim at a stake near saidAlgoods stable and running East fifteen and three fourth poles to a Popular in the Elmore Douglas line thence North four degrees EEast fifteen poles to a Stake on the North sided of the Spring and near the Spring so as to divode the Spring equally between said Douglas and Algood and their Heirs or assigns forever and both the parties are hereby bound never to dig about said Spring so as to alter its present Judit (?) or stop any way to the same or in any other respect to injure said Spring thame North eighty two degrees east two poles to a black gum thence north thirtyf five Degrees East twenty one poles to a Chinquapin white oak thence North thirty threee degrees West twenty six poles to a white Oak thence South thirty and one half poles to a Stake nine poles and three fourths of the Spring thence West fifteen poles and three quarters to a Stake thence North twenty fourPoles to the beginning including four Acres and ywenty one and one fourd ploes be the same more or less which said Tract or parcel of Land with alland every appurtenances thereunto belonging in the siad Elmore Douglas for himself his Heirs executors Administrators or assigns hath hereby should delivered conveyed and confirmed unto the said William Algood his Heirs Executors Administrators or assigns and the said Elmore Douglas doth for himself his Heirs & C. hereby covenant with the said William Algoos his Heirs & C that he said Elmore Douglas his Heirs & C shall and will forever Warrant and defed the said Tract or Parcel Land with all and every member and Appurtenances the unto belonging or in any wise appertaining free from all and every claim or claims of any person or persons what so ever unto the said William Algood his Heirs Executors Administrators or Assigns forever In Witness whereof the sad Elmore Douglas hath hereunto set his Hand and affixed his seal the Day and Date above written Sogned Sealed and Delivered in the Presence of intered the words belonging

Elmore Douglas   (SEAL)

Test S. L. Blakemore
Alstore L. Names
Ennis Douglas
B. Wrather Juyant
Isaas Hearnsderest, Wilson County Court May Term -The mentioned Deed of bergained to William Algood from Elmore Dpuglas for four acres of land was exhibited in open court and proceed by the oaths of Baker Whitker and Isaac Hooks two of the subscribing witness thereunto and ordered to be registered
Test- John Alcorn   Clerk of Wilcosn County (Clk)
State of Tennessee, Wilson County I Henry Ross Reg. of said Coujty do hereby certify that the within Deed is truly registered in Book G. Page (?)---
May 1818   Henry Ross Reg.
Elmore Douglas   To Deed 4 Acres
William Algood   E. M.   Registered Book G. Page

RECORDS OWNED BY MRS. LULA ALGOOD, COOKEVILLE, TENN.

This Indenture made this the thirteenth Day of December in the Year of Our Lord one thousand eight hundred and Sixteen between Benjamin Clak o f the County of Wilson and State of Tennssee of one cart and William Algood of the county and State aforesaid of the other part witness that the Said Benjamin Clark for and in the consideration of the sum of Eighty Dollars to him in Hand paid the Receipt whereof is hereby acknowledged hath bargained sold conveyed and confessed unto the aforesaid William Algood a certain Tract or parcel of Land lying in the County of Wilson and State of Tennesseeand Bounded as follows Beginning on a poplar said Algood South boundry line of a sixty six Acre Tract Purchased of Thomas McClelon and Running on a poplar saidAlgoods South boundry line of a sixty six Acre T act and Running South sixty degrees forty poles East to a stake in Elmers Douglas West boundry line thence North eleven Degrees East twenty poles with said Douglas line to a corner North Poplar East of the Meeting House thence West forty poles to the Beginning including two and one half Acres of Land be the same more or less Which said Tract or parcel of Land with all and every appurtenances thereunto belong the said Benjamin Clark fro himself His heirs Executors Administrator or assignshath sold delivered conveyed and confirmed unto the said William Algood hid heirs Executors Administrators or assugns and the said Benjamin Clark doth fot himself Heirs & Evennly covenant with the said William Algood his Heirs & C that he the said Benjaimn Clark his heirs & C phlland will warrent and forever defend the said tract or parcel of Land with all and every of its membered and Appertenances thereunto belonging any wise Appertaining free from all lawfull claim or claims of any person or persons unto the siad William Algood his heirs Executors Administrators and assignees forever In witness whereof the said Benjamin Clark hath'st his Hand and affixed hisnSeal the day and Date above with signed and sealed and delivered in the presents of Nathan Corley, Samuel Carlinger Jurant at Sept Term 1817

                              Benjamin Clark (Seal)
State of Tennessee Wilson County Court May Term 1819
    The with in Deed ofbargain in Clarks to Wm. Algood for the 2½ acres of land qwas exhibited 12 of Court and fully proved by the oath of Nathm Croley are of the witness thereunto and ordered to be registered
Test   Allcorn Clk. of Wilson County Court
Benjamin Clark To Deeds 2½ acres
  Wm. Algood
        Deed Benjamin Clark
              To
      William Algood

This Indenture made this second Day of June in the Year of Our Lord, one thousand eight hundred and Eighteen between Steven McDaniel of the county of Wilson and State of Tennessee of the one part and William Algood of the county and State aforesaid of the other part witnesseth that the said Stephen McDanial for and ni consideration of the sum of the Seventeen Dollars to him in handnpaid the receipt whereof is hereby acknowledged hath bargained sold conveyed and confirmed unto the siad William Algood a certain tract or parcel of Land lying in the County of Wilson and State of Tennessee adn bounded as follows viz, beginningon a Dogwood said Algood south west corner in said Mc-Danial East boundry line and running East Forty one Poles to a popularin Sd Algood line thence & North twenty Seven Poles to a cornerBeavh in Sd Algood line thence south fifty Degrees West to the beginningin and lying three acres and Seventy three and one half Poles be the came more or less which said Tract or parcel of Land with all and every appertenances thereuntobelonhgig or in any wise appertaining to the said Stephen McDanial for himself Heirs Executors Admijistrators or assigns heth hereby sold delivered conveyed and confirmed unto the sdis William Algood his Heirs Executors Administrators or assigns and the said Stephen McDanial doth hereby for himself his Heirs & C Hereby covenant with th said William Algood hid Heirs & C, that he the said Stephen McDanial hid Heirs & C shall and will warrent and forever defend the said Tract or parcel of Land with all and every of its members and appertenences thereunto belonging or in any wise Appertaining free from all claims of any Person or persons whatsoever un to the said William Algood his Heirs & C forever In witness ahereof the said Stephen McDanial hath seth his hand and affixed his seal the Day and Date above written
Signed Sealed and Delivered in Presance

                                     Stephen McDonald (SEAL)
                                     Acked
John H. Buford   Deed 3 acres
Burchet Douglass   Stephen McDanial
                                       To William Algood R B Page 260

State of Tennessee Wilson County C Court Feb Term 1819
The within Debt of bargain and sale from Stephen McDanial to Wm Algood for was exhibited in open court ask by the said Stephen and ordered to be Registered
Test-   John Alton Clerk
State of Tennessee Wilson County   This Deed is Registered in Book p9 26
                                       Henry Ross Registered

The State of Tennessee
To all to whom these presents shall come Greetings
     Know ye that by virtue of Entry No 131 made in the office of the Entry Taker of Putnam County and Entered on the 3 day of Aprile, 1860 pursuant to the provisions of an Act of the General Assembly of said Satet passed on h the 9th day of January 1830 There is granted bt the State of Tennessee uhto Joel Algood a certain parcel of Land containing Fifty nine acres 3 roads & poles by survey bearing date the 30th day of Aprile 1860lying in the said county on the waters of Falling Waters Beginning at a stake and Blok oaks pointers the South West corner of a tract of Land purchased bt said Algood of James McKinney Running East with his South Bpundry line crossing the

cpuntry Road at 70 poles crossing the Road to the white plains at 16 poles
in all 113 poles to two Chestnuts and 2 Black oaks Algoods corner tnhence
North with another of his lines 51 poles to a stake and 2 Black oaks pointers thence East to poles to a stake in the Road leading to Quarles thence
South 25 East with said Road 53 poles to a stake and 3 Black Jacks pointers thense South qith another of his line 87 poles to 4 post oaks & Black
Jack another of his corners in S. D. Burtons line thence West with his line
36 poles to a Post oak & Black Jack his North West corner South 2 poles to
a stake & Black Jack John W. Welches corner west with his North Boundry line
crossing the Road to White Plains at 46 poles crossing the Cantucky Road at
90 poles inall 110 poles to 4 Black Jacks Welchs corner in John W Shirley
line North with his lines 58 poles to the Beginning with the hereditaments &
and appurtenances To have and To hold the said Tract or parcel of Land with
its appurtenances to the said Joel Algood in witness whereof Isham G.
Harris Gov. of the Sate of Tennessee hath hereunto set his hand and caused
the groat Seal of the State to be affixed at Nashville on 10 day of Apr.
in the Year of Pur Lord one Thousand and Eight Hundred and Sixty one and
of the Independance of the United States the 85 year
                    By the Govnor-Isham G. Harris
                              O. W. R. Ray
                                    Secretary.
Joel Algood is entitled to the within described tract of Land
                              P. P. Trumit
                    per H. T Trumit
Recorded in the office for the Mountain District in Book by page 262
                    Register Mountain District

Grant No 12332
Joel Algood Putnam County 59 a, 3 R 38 pr

RECORDS OF WILSON COUNTY
OWNED BY MRS. ALFRED ALGOOD, COOKEVILLE? TENN.

This in made this twelfth day of November Eighteen hindred and eighteen between George White of Wilson County and State of Tennessee of the one part and Charles ledbeter Hezakiah Woodare and Willis Copied trustees in t trust for the uses and purposes herein mentioned All of the within State of aforesaid George White for and in consideration of the sum of eight dollars specilas to him in hand paid at and upom the sealing and delivering of these presents the receipt whereof is hereby acknowledge hath or have given granted bargained sold released confirmed and convey and bythese presents doth or do give grant bargain sell release confirm and convey un- to them the said Charles Ledbetter Hezakiah Woodard and Willis copied and their successors trustees in trust for the uses and purposes herein after mentioned and declaired all the estate title interest propertyclaim and dem mandwhatsoever either in laws on equiltywhich he the said George White hath or have into or upon all and singular a certain lot or acres of ground sit- uated lying and being in the County and District of bounded and bounded as follows to wit beginning on white aok and Sasafras at the South West corner of said George White's land and running East twenty six poles to a popular tyemce North six and one fourth poles to an sourwood thence west twenty six poles to a stake; thence to the Beginning containing and laid out for one acre of ground to gather with all and singular the houses and woods water ways privileges and appurtenances them to belongingor in any wise appurtain- ing to have and to hold all and singular the above mentioned and described lot or acres of ground situated and lying and being as a foresaid togather with all and singular the houses wood water ways and privileges there to be- longing or in assesingassertaining unto them the said Charles Ledbetter hezakiah woodard Willis copied and their successors in office forever in trust that they shall erect and build or cause to be Erected and built there on a house or place of wirship for the use of the members of the mentioned Episcepel Church on the united State of America according to the rules and disipline which from times to time may agree upon and by ministers and prea- chers of the said Churchtheir general Conferences in the United States of America and in futue trust and confidence that they shall at all times forev erhereafter permits such ministers and preachers belonging to said Churches shall from time to time be duly authorized by the general conferences of th ministers and preschersof the said presches for by the Yearly conferances authorized by the said conferances to preach and expound therein and in further trust and condidence that as often as any one or more of the trustes herein before manticmed shall die or cease to be members of the said church gror dissopline as a foresaid there and in such cases it shall be the duty of Stationed ministers or preachers authorized as before said who shall have the personal charge of the members if the siad church to call a meeting of the remaining trustees as soon as conveniently may be and whenso ever the sa ministers or preacher shall proceed to niminate one or more persons to fill the place or places of him or them whose offuce has or have been vacated as a aforesaid provided the person or persons to nominate shall have been one yea a member or members of the Said church immediately proceeding such nomina- tion and of at least of twenty one years of age and the said trustees so ase sembled shall proceed to Elect and by a majority of votes appointed the per- son or persons so nominated to fill such vacancy ordanesnse in order to keep up the members of hhree trustees forever and in cases of any equal member vote for and against the said mentioned the Stationed ministers or preacher shall have the electing vote provided nevertheless that if the said trustee n any of them or their successors have advanced or shall advance any sum or sums of money or shall be responsable for any sum of money on account of said premises and they said trustees or their successors be obligated to pay the said sum or sums of money they or any party of them shall be authorized to rais the said sum of money by a mortgage on the said premises or by sealing the said premisses of the after notise given to the pastor or preacher who has the oversight of the congregation attending service on the said premises of the money dus be notpaid to the said trustees or their successors with in one year after such notice given and if such sale takes place the said trustees or their successors afterpying the debt and all other expenses which were due from the money arising from such sale shall deposit the remainder of the money prodused by the said sale int the hands successors after paying the debts and all other expenses which are due from the money arising from such sale shall deposite the remainder by the said sale in the hands of the Stewarts of the society belonging to or attending devine service on the said premises which urplus of the produce of such sale so deposited in the hands of the said steward or stewards shall be at the disposal of the next yearly conferanse authorized as aforesaid which said yearly conferance shall dispose og the said momey according to the best of thereJudgment for the use of the said Society and the said George White doth by these presents warrent and forever defend all and Singular the befere mentioned and described lot or acres of ground with the appurtenances thereunto belonging unto them the Said Charles ledbetter Hezakiah Woodward Willis Copied and their suaccessors chosen and appointed as a foresaid from the claimor claims of him the said George White his heirs and assigns foeever Testimony whereof the said George White have had unto set myhand and caused/ seal the day and year a foresaid

George William
Daniel Jackson

Received the day of the date of the above written endenture the considerat#
on ther in mentioned in full
Test, George White (SEAL)
George Williams & Danial Jackson Intrust
State of Tennessee , Wilson County

I Henry Ross Register

I do hereby certify that the White and in duly Registered in Book
H. Page 134 this 24th day of March 1820
Test- Henry Ross Registerof Wilson County
State of Tennessee February Term 1820 Wilson County The within and
of bargain & sale from Georgw White to Charles Ledbetter Hezakiah Woodard
' Willie Cofell was exicuted in open court and Proven by the oaths of
George William and Danial Jackson the subscribing witness thereunto and
ordered by the Court to be Registered
George White (SEAL)   Test- JohnAllcorn Clerk of
                                        Wilson County court
DEED-George White for land to build a meeting house
Registered in Book H. Page 134

RECORDS OF MRS. LULA ALGOOD (CON)

This Indenture made this twentyfourth day of January in the Year of Our Lord Eighteen hundred and twenty four Between Samuel Caplinger of the County of Smith and the State of Tennessee of the one partand William Algood of h theCounty of Wilson and the State aforesaid of the other partWitness thatbth said Samuel Caplinger for and in consideration ofbhe sum of Seventy five dollars and twenty cents to him in hand paid the receipt where of is hereby acknowledged andhimself to be therwith fully satisfied contented and paid Hath given granted bargained soldoffered and conformed unto the said William Algood his heirs ans assigns the following described tract or parcel of land situated in the county of Wilson aforesaid Beginningat a poplar Stump lying and being in the county of Wilsonaforesaid Beginning at a poplar stump South East corner of the tract of landwhere as the saidWilliam Algood now lives Running South fifty degrees East twenty five and one half poles to a stake North West corner of Providence meeting Houselot therewith seventy seven degrees East with the north Boundry line of siad lot Eleven poles to a Stake Thence North six degreesWest Douglas line sixteen poles thence North ten degreesEast with said line ten and one half poles 24 links tea stake thence North 62 West with the south boundry line of the tract whereonthe said Algood now lives forty poles to a Stake thence West to afores aid place Beginning 34 poles containing nine acres and 64 square poles to have and to hold the above described parcel of land with its appertenances to the said William Algood his heirs and assigns and the said Samuel Caplinger doth further consort compromiseand assign to and with the said William Algood that he the said Samuel Caplinger his heirs and assigns will forever warrent and defend to the said Algood his heirs and the aforesaid tract of Land with all the Appertenances thereunto belonging ahainst the aforesaid tract of Land with all and every person or person in the within whereof shall hereto set my hand and affixed my seal the day and date above written signed sealed and delivered in the presence of

          Burchett Douglas (Juror)
          Moody P Hail
          Lewis Harris J rant
          Samuel Caplinger (Xhis mark)
             (SEAL)

State of Tennesse Wilson County Court June Term 1824
The with in deed of bargain and sale from Samuel Caplinger to William Algood for nine acres -poles of land was produced in open court andn proven by hhe Oath of   Burchett Douglas &
          Lewis Harris Subscribing witness

thereto and ordered to be Registered

          Neil John Alcorn Clk of said County

In the office the 29th July, 1824

          H. ,Ross Register
Tennessee, I, Henry Ross Reg, of Wilson Co. do hereby certify the the within deed and certificate proven thereon and Registered
Deed 9. A. 64 P.
Samuel Caplinger
  Deed To William Algood
  & -64
  E. M. Registered in Book No Page 125

RECORDS OWNED BY MRS. LULA ALGOOD, COOKEVILLE, TENN.

This Indenture made the Twenty Second Day of Oct. one thiusand eight
hundred and twenty four between Willis Cofeld of the County of Wilson and
State of Tennessee of the one part ofWilliam Algood of the County of state
aforesaid of the other part Witnesseth that hte said Willis Cofeld for and
in consideration of the sum of two hundred and fifty Dollars to him in had
paid the receipt whereof is whereby acknowledged with granted bargained and
sold and delivered and by these presents doth grant bargain sell and deliver unto the said William Algood his Heirs Exens Administrators or assigns
a certain Tract or Parcel of Land situated lying and being in the cpunty
of Wilson on the waters of Cedar Creek containing Sixty ywo Acres be the sm
same more or less neginning at a Cedar N. W. at corner of a survey of Danial
McKesicks and RunningWest 34 poles to a Stake thenceNo C. poles to a Sassafrs
thence South & 5 Degrees West 45 poles to a stake thence 2½ poles to a stek
thence West 27 Poles to a white oak and Sassafras, thence South 105 poles
toa cedar thence East 110 poles to a stake thence North th the begin ning
which peace or parcel of Land with all the apertenances and improvements
thence unto belonging or in any wise appertaining the said Willis Cofeld
for himself his Heirs exetrs administrators orassigns doth forever warreht
and defend the title against the claims of all and every preson or persons
what so ever to the sdis William Algood his Heirs Exers Sdmins or assigns
forever , In witness where of the said Willis Cofeld hath unto set his Hand
and affixed hisSeal the day and date above mentioned . Signed Sealed and
delivered in the presents of
Samuel T. White   Lurary Woods Clk Jurant   SEAL
Ennis Douglass Jurant
State of Tennesse Wilson County Court, March Term 1825
Bargain & Sale from Willis Coffeld to William Algood for 60 acres of land
was duly proven in open court by the oaths of James Woodcock & Ennis Douglas
two of the Subscribing witness thereto and ordered to be Registered.
                                         Alcorn Clerk
                    Frisk John of said Court
Tennessee Wilson County, I, Henry Ross Register of said County do hereby
certify that the weather report and probate are duly Registered in my office
this 9th day of May 1825
                    Test-Henry Ross Regs.

Deed from Cofeld to
Willaim Algood 26 acres
Registers in Book K, Page 355

RECORDS OF MRS. LULA ALGOOD, COOKEVILLE, TENN.

State of Tennessee No 8833-
To all to whom these present shall come Greetings- Know ye, that by virtue
of Entry No 1804 made in the office of the Entry Taker of Overton County an
and entered on the 6th day of May 1842 pursuant tot eh provisions fo an Act
of the General Assembly of said State passe don the 9th day of January 1830
there is Grantee by the said State of Tennessee unto enry McKinlwy a certain tract or parcel of Land containing firty Eigth acres by survey bearing
date the 66ht day of May 1842 lying in said County abthe Waters of Bear Crek
Beginning at a post aak two Spanish Oak pointers the North West corner of
C Carr, Tract on which the said McKinley now lives Running East with the
Noth boundry of said tract one hindred and six poles to a hickory and points
corner to saidMcKinleys two hundred acre Tract Then North with the same
sixty six poles to a chestnut and four Black oaks pointers Burton Marchbanks
corner Thence West with said line one hundred and sixteen poles to a post oak
and two Hickory pointers Marchbanks coener Thence South with John Douglas
line sixty five poles to a hickory Thence East ten poles to the beginning
with the hereditaments and Appurtenences to have and to hold the siad tract
or parcel of Land with its appurtenences to the said Henry McKinley.
In witnes s whereof James C. Jones Govnor of the State of Tennessee has
hereunto set his hand and caused the Great Seal of the State to be affixed
at Nashvielle, on the 20th day of Aprile 1843 and of America Independance
the 67th year.

                                        James C. Jones Gov.
                                        Jon. S. Young, secretary.

Henry McKinley is entitled to the within described land.
                        R. Nelson, Register of the Mountain District
Recorded in my Office Book L. page 278-279
                                Nelson Register of the Mountain Dis.
                                By W. E. Nelson, D. R.

No 8833 Henry McKinney 48 acres
        Overton County.

                                Ashgrove- Aprile 21st, 1845
    I was called on with T. W. Fits of Summer County to settle a disputed
line between Joel Algood and Wm. L. John P and Gideliah Hughes and after ex-
amining the boundry of the two tracts and the title papers and taking evidene
of John Bell, Elijah Jones and George Martin upon oath came to the conclusion that the line that Algood claims was the original line and the line
that the former owners of the land claimed to and Jurisdiction to and acknowledged to be the line for many years Given under my hand this date above
written.
                                T. E. Morris

I, Zealous Johnson Administrator P. C of William Swinney deceased do hereby virtue of the power in me vested by law and in complyance with the last will and testament of said William Swinney convey hereby to Joel Algood he being the highest and best bidder for the consideration of two hundred and eighty two dollars and sixty cents to me this day paid by said Algood a tract of land in the Satet of Tennessee Wilson County District No. 7 containing by estimation thirty acres and one hundred and forty two poles be the same more or less and boundee as follows Beginning at a rock Bryans Wards corner with an Elm Black and White oak pointer and running thence South with the said Wards west boundry seventy six and three quarter poles to a stake and R hickory and Blck Locust pointers it being the North East corner of the tract willed by the said Swinney to his widow thence West seventy nine and a half poles with said widows North boundry to a stake in the East boundry of the heir of W. W. Calhan deceased Thence North with thw road from Taylorville to McCalitus fifty three poles to a stake Thence East fifty seven and a half poles to a Hickory Thence North twenty one poles to a sugar tree on said road Thence East one poles to the beginning The title to which land I here bind the heirs of the said William Sweeney to warrent and defend tot eh said Algood against the lawful claims of all persons are fully and effectually as their could be bounded if the said Sweenying had executed this deexd himself according to the power invested Given under my handand sael this 20th day of August

                                        Zealous Johnson Adms of this surveyed
Deed   SEAL
Signed sealed & delivered in our presence the day and date above written
                        J. T. Bell proven 1856
                        J. R. Beachen

State of Tennessee Wilson County Personaly appeared before me Joseph L. McClain clerk of the county Court of said County of Wilson Zealous Johnson the within named Administrator a bargainer with whom I am personally acquahted and whom acknowledged that he executed the within Deedfor the purpose therein contained witness my hand at office this forst day
                                        J. L. McClain Clerk

Deed- Z. Johnson Adm PC
      To
Joel Algood 30 acres , 142 poles
Proved by B. T. Bell Sept, 1, 1856 Act Sept 1856
Revd for Registration Sept 1, 1856 at 12, O'clock W
                                        A. W. Vick Reg

State Tax 5.
Reg fee   1.00 paid
Clerk fee   25

          132

DEED
OWNED BY MRS. LULA ALGOOD, COOKEVILLE, TENN

I L. White Trustee for Edward White this day bargained and sold and do hereby transfer and convey to Joel Algood an his heirs forever for the consideration of Three thousand and two hundred and seventy five Dollars to me paid one lot in the town of Lebanon representatives in the plot of said Town as lot No 6 also one other lot representative of lot No 7 in the North Square of said Town boundry ob the South by the land that Jno. M. Goldron n lives on an the lot belonging to John Hoolman on the east by Academy street an on the West by Main North Street & on the North by two acres of land the residence of the said E. A. White said lots are conveyed to E. A. WHite by Albert H. Wayman and Fly Crutcher and Monroe D ouglas also lot or parcel of land bounded as follows Beginning at the North West corner of lot N . running North to to the said South West corner of George Donwalls lot thence east with said Donnells line on the school lands to the street thence South with Academy Street to the North Corner of lot No 7, thence West wit h the boundry of lots No 7 to the beginning about two acres it being the place Whom the said E. A. White now lives also the one half of an hundred tract of land lying in the County of Wilson and State of Tennessee on the water Cedar Creek for the consideration of four hindred dollars to me paid the said land is bounded as follows on the North by the land of Henderson Holey on the East by the land of H. Y. Massa on the South by the lands of Daniel Johnson on the Wesy by the lands of Daniel Johnson and Samuel Capner the whole of said tract of land is estimated to containing two hundredand ten acres said land was debted to White and Price by William Johnson theone half of the above mentioned two hundred and ten acres is hereby conveyed tot the saod Joel Algood to have and to hold the above describeed Town property and tract of land to said Joel Algood his heirs and assghs forever I the said L. W. WHiteTrustee for said do covenent with the said Joel Algood, th I am lawfully seized of said land and town property, have a good right to convey it and that the same is unincumbered I do further covenant and bind myself my heirs and representatives as trustee of aforesaid to warrent and forever defend the title to the above described property portion thereof to the said Joel Algoodhis heirs and assigns against the lawful claims of all persons whatsoever this the 8th day of December on ethousnad eight hundred and forty one the above dollars entitles before signed

S. W. White, Trustee (SEAL)

for E. A. White & I. W. White
State of Tennessee Wilson County Personally appeared before me Josiah McClain Clerk of the County Court of said Wilcsn County the with in L. W. White whthh whom I am personally acquainted and acknowledged that executed the with in deed for the purpose therein contained Witness my hand at office this 8th day of December 1841

J. T. McClain Clerk

State of Tennessee I Giles Glenn Register of Wilson County do hereby certify that the within deed and certificate ofacknowledgment thereon duly Registered in my office in Book F. Page 397 witness my hand at office this 15th day of December A. D. 1841

Giles H. Glenn Reg.

L. W. White
    Deed
Joel Algood
Register Fee 1.75

RECORDS OF MRS. LULA ALGOOD (CON)

I bind myself to pay John White eight hundred and thirtyeight dollars
The condition of this obligation is such that whereas the said John White
has this day purchased of me four hundred and eighteen dollars and seventy
cents on the following payments and third due July 1st 1845 , 1st July
1846 and C due third July 18st, 1847 for which note underseal have been this
day executed to me a tract of land in Wilson County State of Tennessee
District No 7 and biunded as follows Beginning at a hickory Marchsuns
South West corner in B. T. Billsworth boundry Thence North sixty poles o
to two Hickorys and two Beeches Thence West forty poles to a mulberry and
sugar tree Thence South fifty fourdegrees West thirty five poles to a
white oak and poplar Thence West thirty four poles to a stake a little
north of a branch Thence South fifty and a half degrees West twenty seven
poles to a walnut Thence South twenty poles to a beech and C. two Hickory
Thence South sixty four degrees West forty poles tema Hickory Black Gum
and Dogwood Thence Southtyo and a half degrees West tyirty two poles to
a Black and White Oak and Elm Thence East ninty two poles to a Black walnut B. T. Bell south west corner Thence north one degree East with Bairs
Nells west boundry forty poles to a Ironwood and Hickory said Bells norh
west corner Thence East seventy poles to the beginning Law if I shall mk
make or cause to be made to the said John White his heirs or assigns a good
and sufficient title in fee simple with generly wardly to the said tract o
of land on the making of last paymentthere this obligation to be void
This November 7th 1844

                                                    Joel Algood (SEAL)

Test-A. J. McDonald, Ben. T. Bell

Bond -Joel Algood To John White 62¾ acres

I, Joel Algood dind myself to pay Benjamin T. Bell nine hundred and
twenty dollars . The condition of this obligation is such that whence the
said Benjamin T. Bell has this day purchased for me the same of four hun-
sixty dollars on the following payments One hundred and fifty three dollars
and 33¼ due on the 25th day of January 1852The same amount due on the 25th
day of January 1854 & the for which his notes under seal have this day
been executed to me a tract of Land in the State of Tennessee Wilson County
District Np 7 containing by estimation sixty two acres and one hundred and
twenty poles be the same more or less and bounded as follows to wit: Beginning at a Hickory in said Bells South boundry which is W. M. Calahan sohh
west corner and running thence North west corner Thence West forty poles
to a mulberry and sugar tree Thence South fifty four degrees west thirty
five poles to a white oak & poplar Thence West thirty four poles to a stak
near a branch Thence South fifty & a half degrees west twenty semen poles
to a walnut and said branch thence South twenty poles toa beach & hickory
Thencesouth sixty four degrees west forty poles to a Hickory Black Gum & D
Dogwood Thence South two and a half degrees west th rty two poles to a blac
and white oak & Gum Thence East ninty two poles to a small Black walnut
said Bells south west corner Thence North one degree East forty poles to
an ironwood & Gickory thence west seventy poles to the beginning now if I
shall make or cause to make to the said Benjamin T. Bell his heirs and
assignd a good right and sufficient title in fee simple with general

RECORDS OF MRS. LULA ALGOOD, (CON)

waranty to the said tract of land an the making of last payment then this
obligation to be void This day 25th of January 1851

James Joel Algood (SEAL)

Entitle before assigned
Test-,E. P. Low, G. A. duncan

State of Tennessee—No 8833.
To all to whom shall presents shall come Greeting: Know ye That by virtue
of Entry No 1804 made in the office of the Entry Taker of Overton County
and entered on the 6th day of May 1842 pursuant to the provisions of an
Act of the General Assembly of said State passed on the 9th day of January
1830 there is Granted by the said State of Tennessee unto Henry McKinley
a certain tract or parcel of land containing forty eight acres by survey
bearing date the 6th day of May 1842 lying in said county on the waters of
Bear Creek Beginning at a post oak two Spanish oaks pointers the north
west corner of C. Garve Tract on which the said McKinley now lives Running
East withthth North boundry of said tract one hindred and six pales to a
hickory and pointer corner to said McKinneys two hundred acre Tract Then
North with the same sixty six poles to a chestnut and four Black oaks pointers Burton Marchbanks corner Thence West with the said line and one hundred and sixteen poles to a post Oak and two hickory pointer Marchbanks coener The ce South with Jihn Douglas line sixty five poles to a hickory Thene
East Teh poles to thebeginning with the hereditaments and Appurtenences to
have and to hold the said tract or parcel of Land with its appurtenences
to the slaid Henry McKinny In witness whereof James C. Jone Govnor of the
State of Tennessee has hereunto set his hand and caused the Great Seal of th
State to be affixed at Nashville on the 20th day of Aprile 1843 and of
America Independance the 67th year

James C. Jones
Jon. S. Young Secretary

Henry McKinney is entitled to the within described land

R. Nelson Register of the Mountain
District

Recorededim my office Book L. Pages 278-279

Nelson Register of the Mountain District
by W. E. Nelson, D. R.

No 8833
Henry McKinny 48 acres
Overton County

RECORDS OF MRS. LULA ALGOOD (CON)

I, John L. Dillard have this day bargained and sold and do hereby transfer and convey to Joel Algood and his heirs foeever for the consideeeration of five hundred abd forty six dollars a tract of land in the State 66 Tennessee Wilson County District No 7 containing by estimation ninty five acres be the same more or less and boundes as follows Beginning on a Black oak said Algoods North East coener of a tract of land purchased by William Algood of Benjamin Clark and running thence South eighty seven degrees west one hundred and forty two poles to a large white oak and Beach said Algoods South West corner of tract above named bought of Clark Thence North forty seven degrees West twenty six and a half opoles to a stake a large white oak and Beach said Algoods South West corner of a tract abovenamed bought of Clark Thence North forty seven degrees West twenty six and a half poles te a stake a large white oak and small walnut and Hiskory pointers Yhence Norh two degrees East two hundred and four poles to a stake two ash and two locust pointers Thence North forty five degrees East fifty seven poles te a beach and Hickory on the road lead from Hart Ferry to Road Thence South seventeen degreed East two poles to a stake Thence South forty eight degrees East seventy four poles to the boundry of Providence Camp ground Thene with the west and south boundry of said Camp ground to the South East coener of said ground Thence South five degrees east about sevnentynpoles to a sti Burch and sugar tree pointers Thence South seventy degreesEast forty poles t the beginning To have and to hold the same to the said Joel Algood his heirs and assigns forever I do covenant with the said Algood that I am lawfully seized if said land have agood right to survey it and that the asame is unincumbered I do further covenent and bind myself my heirsand representative forever to warrent and defend the title t to the said land and my part thereof to the said Algood his heirs and assigns against the lawful claims of all persons This Nov, 9th 1844

Test- A. J. McDonald   J. L. Dillard (SEAL)
      John J. Dillon

State of Tennessee Wilson County Personally appeared before me Josiah L. McClain clerk of the County Court if said Wilson County A. J. McDonald and John Dillon subscribing witness to the within and who being sworn depose and say they are acquainted with the named Jihn L, Dillard the bargner with whom I am (?) and that he acknowledged the same in their presence to be his act & deed upon the day it bears date witness jy hand at office this 27th day of January 1845

                                                    J. L. McClain Clerk

State of Tennessee Wilson County , I, A. W. Vick Registrr of Wilson County do certify that the within Deed and certificate are duly Recorded in my office in Book V. Page 182-183 January 28th 1845 at 1 OClock P. M.

                                                    A. W. Vick Register

Deed
J. L. Dillqrd
    To
Joel Algood
Clerks Fee   .25
State tax   .14
         - -----
         paid 394
Rec for Registration January 28th, 1845 at 1' oclock P. M.
                    A. W. Vick Reg
                    fees 1.00 by A. Algood

RECORDS OF MRS. LULA ALGOOD (CON)

I, John J. Selvy have this day bargained and sold and do hereby transfer and convey to Joel Algood his heirs and assigns for the consideration of one hundred and ninty dollars to me paid a tract of land in the State of Tennessee Putnam County District No 1 containing by estimation thirty eight acres be the same more or less and bounded as follows to wit: Beginning on the South West corner of a twenty acre tract conveyed by me to said Algood the 27th of November last and running thence west sixty ywo and a half poles to two chestnut pointers eight or ten poles South of Burtons Harps south east corner Thence North nine degrees west and with said Harps east boundry line eighty poles to three Black oaks and a post oak pointer Thence East seventy five and a half poles to the North West coener of said twenty acre tract Thence North fifteen and a half poles to a small Black Jack Chestnut and Hickory pointer Thence east forty poles the south west coener of a five hundred and fifty acre tract conveyed by James McKinley to said Algood Thence South fifteen and a half poles to a Black Gum pointer Thence West forty poles to two small Persimmons pointers Thence South eightympoles to the beginning to have and to hold the same to the said Algood his heirs and assigns forever I do covenent with the Algood that I am lawfully seized of said land have a good right to convey it and that the same is unincumbered I d do further covenent and bind myself my heirs and representatives forever to warrent and defend the title to the said land and every part thereof to the said Algood his heirs and assigns against the lawful claims af all persons This day of December 1858

John J. Selvy (SEAL)

Test-I. W. Crutcher, R. B. McD nial, Loyd S. Selvy
State of Tennessee Putnam County Personally appeared before me Russell Moore Clerk of Putnam County Cpurt John J. Selvy the within bargainer with whom I am personally acquainted and who acknowledged the due Execution of the within deed of conveyance to be his act and deed for the purpose and things Therein contained which is recorded witnessed my hand at office the 27th day of December 1858

Russell Moore Clerk

State of Tennessee Putnam County , I, Steven W. Brown Register of said county do hereby certify that the within deed of conveyance was filed for Registration on the 28th day of Dec. 1858 & was noted on filation Book A. pg 82-82 at 3 o'clock P. M. and was Registered on Book C. Pages 135% 136

S. W. Brown
Register

Deed
J. J. Selvy
    To
Joel Algood 38 acres
State Tax   5.00
Clerks fee   .25
Reg. fee   1.05

Ack 27th Dec. 1858

RECORDS OF MRS. LULA ALGOOD, (CON)

The State of Tennessee-
To all to whom these presents shall come Greetings:

Know ye that in consideration of Intry No 1612 Made into the office
of the Entry Taker of Overton County and entered on the 1st day of May 183
1837 Pursuant to the provisions of an Act of General Assembly of said
State passes on 9th day of January 1830 Therenis Granted by the said State
of Tennessee unto William Terry assigned of James Peek a certain Tract or
Parcel of Land containing Thirty acres by Survey bearing date the Fifteenth day of January 1839 lying in Overton County on the waters of Bear Creek
Beginning at a small hickory and three white oaks pointer the North East corn
of a fifty acre Survey made in the namr of Robert Peek and now owned by
James Peek Running nine and one half poles to a smallBlack oak a post
oak and two black oak pointers corner to Henry Brewington fifty acrevTract
Thence West with the same one hundred and ten poles to a black oak on the b
banks of Bear Creek in a line of Robett Peeks Tract South with the same
seventeen poles to a stake and white oak pointer corn to the same West
seven and a fourth poles to a stake South ninty two and one half poles to
a Stake a blck oak and hickory pointer East thirty three poles to a stake
a hickory post oak and black oak Saplin pointer Northpassing the Siurth West
corner of said Peek's fifty acre tract at two poles and with the same in all
one hundred and two poles to a hickory Peeks corn East with the same fifty p
poles to the Beginning with the hereditaments and appurtenances To have and
To hold the said Tract or Parcel of Land with its appurtenances to the said
William Terry and his heirs forever In witness whereof Neil S Brown, Govnor of the State of Tennessee hath hereunto set his hand andcaused the Great
Seal of the State to be affixed at Nashville on the Twenty fifth day of
August in the Year of Our Lord one Thousand eight hundred and forty nine
and of the Independance of the United States and Seventy Fourth year

W. B. A. Murmsey
By the Governor N. T. Brown

William Terry is entitled to the within Described tract o;f Land

Jno F. Vass Register Mountain District

Recorded in the Registers office for the Muntain District in Book W. Page
137   JohnFT Vass Rigister Mountain District
No 10119William Terry 311 acres Overton County

WILL
RECORD OWNED BY MRS. LULA ALGOOD, COOKEVILLE, TENN.

State of Tennessee Wilson County. At a circuit court of the Fifth Juducial circuit began and held in and for the County aforesaid at the Court House in the town of Lebanon on the third Monday in January in the Year of Our Lord Eighteen hundred and fifty three and of America Independance the 77th President the Hon. Hughes L. Davidson , Judge of said Court Squire Potts vs Joel Algood Come the parties by there Attornies and thereupon came a jury of good and lawful men to wit James B Thomas 1 W. J. Cragwall 2 Jonathan Eatherly 3, L.W. Robertson 4 Richard Hollaway 5 W. B. Jennings 6 Larance Sypert Robert Johnson 8 Guy J Cleaves 9 G Edemound Gilliam Jonathan F. Heckory 11 and Joseph Johnson who being elected tried and sworn the truthto sapek upon the issue joined on there oaths do say tha the proper writing in the pleadings mentioned is not the last will and testament of Elizabeth Algood deceased. It is therefore consideredby the court that the said paper writing August 12, 1848 is not the last will and testament of the said Elizabeth AlgoodIt is therefore considered by the Court thatbthe defendant recover of the Plaintiff the costs of this suit and that exedutors issue AC Squire Potts VS Joel Algood Be it remembered that this course come on this day 12th January 1853 to be heard before the Hon. H. L. Davidson Judge and a jury where the plaintiff introduced Andrew J. M. McDonald one of the subscribing witnesses to the paper writing purporting to be the last will and testament of Elizabeth Algood deceased, who stated that he had been acquainted with Elizabeth Algood for a great many years He signed a paper at the request of Mrs. Algood and which she said was her act and deed. The paper was folded partly he did not read it nor did she say what it was. Nothing more was saidabout a will at the time he signed it. The paper writing purporting to be thw will was there shown to him and he said that his name signed as witness there to was his handwriting and he supposed it was the same he had signed at her request. At the time he sogned her name as witness to the paper he thought she was of sound mind He had but little conversation with her at the time nor at any other since then he has heard read the paper purposing to be her will and has seen a copy of the will of William Algood her husband and seeing that she had willed away property that did not belong to her He had his doubts wheather shw was of sound mind at the time when he witnessed the paper that Joel Algood her son was always very kind and affectionate to his mother as far as he knew The Plaintiff than introduced Jacob S. Horn the other witness to the paper, who stated t thathe had known Elizabeth Algood a great many years and for the last twenty yearsbefore her death he had visited her at least once a year at her request he had witnessed the paper writing purporting to be her will now produced She said it was her will is not certain that he read it but thinks he did She said her husband in his life time had said that the Negro woman Jane had come by her and wants to be permited to labor for herself. She called him into the Garden and seemed disposed to be very secret he thinks he signed his name in the garden, he conversed with her on religious subjects She said she was seeking sanctification of her soul and ask him to pray that she moght obtain that grace. She would frequently repeat the same tha things over and thought she talked foolish from these two last facts and her Disposition to be very secret and from the contexts of the will itself he had his doubts as to wheather she was a sound mindat the time he witness the paper the Plaintiff then ceased his indeir and by consent was permittd

to read to the jury the paper writing purporting to be the last will and
testament of Elizabeth Algoodselest to exceptions The Defendantthen introduced Dr. Regin Thompson a practicing Physician who stated that he had
known Mrs. Algood for twenty years before her death Saw her frequently for
the first two years of his acquaintance butnot so frequently for the last
tenyears of his life She had consulted him about a mole on his face think-
ing it would turn to be a cancer. He assured her here was no danger, thati
was nothing but a mole During the first of the his acquaintance with her
this assurance seemed to satisfy her but during the last ten years of her
life she consulted him about the mole every time he saw her and would ask
about it several times during the same conversation seeming to forget she
had mentioned it before she would also consult him about her negroes but pw
partisularly about a woman named Mary In the same conversation shw would
repeat over the same question and after he had told herwhat she wanted to
knew she would follow when he started off and after he had gotten on his
horse would some times detain him an hour asking him the same questions she
had asked him just before She had a parcel of old medicine wraped up in old
paper She would get this out and show them to him and ask him what they were
good for He told her they were no account and advised her to threw them in h
the fire She would fold them carefully and put them away The next time he
would visit her the same thing would occur in regard to the medicine When
there she slept in a little room with a great many shelves in it having on
them a great anny articles and among them rest a variety of victuals that
seemed to be old and had been there a long time When he would start off she
would insist upon him to take some biscuit and would give him some old hard
dry biscuits that no person could eat He called there one night in the ab-
sence of her Son Joel and she seemed to be alarmed and asked why he had come
there after night She seemed to be so much alarmed that he left and went to
a neighbors house and stayed all night He was related to her by marriage and
she seemed to have confidence in him This seemed about four years before ha
death. From all the circumstances and from her appearance he is satisfied
that she had for ten years before death been of unsound mind that the reason Judgment and memory had been declining that she was very old when she d
died which hapened in January 1852 That a neat tombstone had been put over
the grave of her husbandseveral years before her death This was done shortly
after his deathand before the date of the will This was all the proof in the
cause. The Court charged the Jury that if he believed that Elizabeth Algood
was of sound mind and deposing mind   memoryat the time the paper purporting to be her will was witnessed it would be her will and to find for the
plaintiff but if the proof did not show that she was of sound mind and disposing mind and memory at the time it was witnessed It would not be herw wil
and they ought to find against it and in favor of the defendant and that
how the facts where they must Judge from the proof. This is in Substance
the charge without stating it fully. The Jury returned a verdict for the defendant. The Statement of the proof in the cause and the proceeding had there
in made and signed by the presiding Judges and orderee to be spread upon the
minutes of the Court ay the request of Joel Algood the defendant in this
H. L. Davidson (SEAL)

State of Tennessee Wilson County I Calvin W. Jackson Clerk of the Circuit
Court for the county of Wilson I state aforesaid do hereby cert fy that the
foregoing is a true and perfect copy of the Judgment in th case heretofore
prosecuted and delivered in said court wherein Squire Potts, Plaintiff and J
Jole Algood Deft and the evidence in said cause as the same remain of recon-
ed in my office Witness my hand at office the 11th Oct 1853
C. W. Jackson Clk

RECORDS OF MRS. LULA ALGOOD, (CON)

I, James McKinney have this day bargained and sold and do hereby transfer and convey to Joel Algood and his heirs and assigns for the consideration of Twenty seven Hundred and fifty dollars to me payed a tract of land &
in the State of Tennessee Putnam County District No 1 on both sides of the road leading from Sparta to Livingston containing by estimation five hundred and fifty acres be the same more aorless and biunded as follows, Beginning on a post oak one of Steven Burtons corner in his North boundry andu running thence West one Hundred and thirty eight poles to a stake and thence to Post oak pointers on the esat side ofma glade Thence North fofrty poles te the road Quarles Thence North twenty five degrees West with said road fifty three poles to a stake Thence West ten and a half poles te a stake and Bkack Jackaand Black Oak pointer Thence South twenty eight poles to.a Stake and chestnut Post Oak and Black oak pointers Thence West crossing the road leading to Livingston one hundred and seventeen poles to a stake and Black Oak pointer in John Salbys east boundry Thence North eighty eight poles to a sth stake and Black oak and Black Jack pointers Thence East one hundred and seven poles to a Stake Thence North one hundred and eighty poles to a Stake and Hickory and bkack oak Pointers Thence West eighty poles to two white oaks Thence North one hundred and eleven poles to a smallpost oak and Black gum Thence East eighty poles to two Small beach oaks Thence South and eighteen poles to a Hickory Poast OakMarsh BanksSouthWest corner Thence East one hundred and sixteen poles crossing the Road leading to Livingston to four Black oaks Thence North five poles to a post Oak and Hickory Thence East sixty two poles to a Hickory and post Oak thence SouthThirty seven poles to a stake Thence East fifty poles to a stake Thence South twenty poles to a s take Thence East one hundred poles to a Spanish Oak and two Chestnuts pointers Thence South one hundred and thirty poles to a Post Oak and Black Gum Thence West two hundred and thirty six poles to a Black and P st oak Thence South twenty two degrees East forty four poles to a Black and post oak Thence South fifty degrees East thirty poles to a Walnut Thence South fory five degrees West six and a half poles to twoBkackmoaks Thence South thirty a nine Degrees East twelve poles to the BeginningTo have and to hold the same to the siaid Algood his heirs and assigns forever I do covenant with the said Algood that I am lawfully seized of said land have a good right to convey it and that the same is unincumbered I dofurther covenant and bind myself my heirs and representatives to warrent and defend the title to the said land and every part thereof to the said Algood his heirs and assigns against the Lawful claims of all persons This day of Aprile 1858
                                                                SEAL

(THE end of this one)

This Indenture made this day 22 of Oct, Eighteen hundred and twenty four between William Dillard of the County of Wilson and State of Tennessee of the one part and William Algood of the county and state aforesaid of the other part witnesseth that the said William Dillard and for consideration of the sum of two hundred and twenty five Dollars to him in Hand paid the Receipt whereof acknowledged hath granted bargained sold and delivered and by these presents doth grant bargain sell and deliver unto the Said William Algood his heirs Exor, Administrators or assigns a certain tract or parcel of Land situayed lying and being in the county of Wilson on the waters of Cedar Creek containing forty six acres and sixtypoles beginning at a Red bud and white Oak in George Bradleys North West corner running 126 poles to a cedar Thence East 6 ½ poles to a stake thence South to an ironwood and Elm on a Branch proceeding from a Pondjust above thence with the meaders of a Branch down to a barnbeam thence South 78 Degrees West to the beginning containing 46 acres and 60 poles be the same more or less which piece or parcel of Land with all and every improvement and appertance of Land with all and and evrery improvement and appertenance therein to belonging or in any wise appertaining the said William Dillard hath hereby Should for himself his Heirs Exor, Administrators or assigns and doth forever wacrrentd and defend the title of said Land unto theSaid William Algood his heirs Exors adm or assign free from all and every claim or claims of any person p or persons what so ever to the onlyuse and behalf of him the Sd William Algood his Heirs Exors Administ or assigns forever
In witness where of the Said William Dillard hath hereunto Set his Hand and affixed his Seal the day and date above written or mentioned
Signed Sealed and delivered in presents of

William Dillard (SEAL)

Jurat- Ennis Douglas
James W. Adcock

DEED   NO 113

Joel Algood enters Three hundred acres of land in Putnam County on the waters of the Falling waters Beginning on John J. Srlys South East corner at and running thence West with his line Thence South Thence East Thence North With Stephen D. Burton's west boundry of said Algoods South bpundry Thence with said line to said Seleys East boundry Thence South with his East boundry to the Beginning

This July 13, 1858
Joel Algood Locator

A copy Tast
Jon Buck Jr.
Entry Taker of Putnam County

DEED
RECORDS OF MRS. LULA ALGOOD (CON)

Deed- Made to A. J. McDonald who purchased of W. F. Sept 7th 1853 I witnessed by said Bell & Wm Dillard I bind myself to pay William T Bell four
hundred and sixteen dollars The consideration of the obligation such that
whereas the said Bell for this day purchased of me for two hundred and
eight dollard and sixty five cents on the following payments to wit one
hundred andfifty four dollars the 25 day of December next and fofty four
dollars andsix ty five cents on the 25 day of January 1853 which his note
under seal have this day Exerated to me a tract of land in the State of
Tennessee Wilson County District bounded as follows Beginning on a black p
and white oak & a black Gum in Elijah Johns North boundry and thence East
seventy two poles to a dogwood and Box Elder Thence North two degrees wast
thirty one poles to two ten pointers in a hollar Thence west twelve poles
to two poplars pointers Thence forty and a half degrees West thirty poles
to a sugar treenThence South fourteen poles to a Semall Black Walnut on a
large Branch Thence South seventy five degrees West twenty poles down said
branch Thence North sixty four degrees W st with said branogh twelve poles
Thence West four and a half poles to a Stake in Dwid Wheeler East boundry
Thence South two and a half degrees west ninty two poles to the beginning
containing twenty three acres and twenty and nine poles be the same more or
less if I should make or cause to be made to thesaid Wm h s heirs or assigns
a good and sufficient title in the simple with general warrentty on the
making of the past payment Then this obligation to be void ThisNov the 1st
1857

                          H. Tinsley Bond-
                          B. T. BEll Sam A. Algood
                                  To Wm T. Bell
                          23 acres deed made to A. J. McDonald
who purchased of W. T. Bell Sept. 7th 1853

    I William Terry I have this day Bargained and sold and hereby transfer
and convey to James McKinley and his heirs forever for the consideration
of Twenty five Dollars to me paid a tract of land in the State of Tennessee
Overton County and District number 1 containing by estimation Th rty acres
be the same more or less and bounded as follows on the waters of Bear Creek
Beginningat a small Hickory and three white oaks pointers the North East
corner of a fifty acre survey made in the name of Robert Peek and nowowned
by said William Terry running nine and one half poles toma small Black oak
a post Oak and two Black oaks pointers corner to Henry Brewingtons fifty
Acre tractthence West with the same one hundred poles to a Black oak on the
Banks of Bear Creek in a line of Robert Peeks tract south with the same
seventeen poles to a stake south ninety two and one half poles to a stake
a Black oak and Hickory pointers thence East thirty three poles to a stake
a Hickory post oak and Black oak saplins pointers thence North passing
theSouth west corner of said fifty acres tract at two poles and with the sm
same in all one hundred and two poles to a Hickory Peeks corner East with
the same fifty poles to the Beginning To have and to hold the same to the &
said James McKinny his heirs and assigns forever I do covenant and bind myself my heirsand Representatives to warrent and defend the title of said
land to James McKinney his heirs and assigns forever against and claims tob
be madeby myself or any person claiming through or under me but nofurther

RECORDS OF MRS. LULA ALGOOD (CON)

this day of August 1850

William Terry (Xhis mark) SEAL

Attest
D. W. Hawes
S. D. Burton
Jonathin Fowler

William Terry
        To Deed 50 acres
James M. McKinley

Lebanon June 21st 1865

Mrs. Nancy Algood,
Madam!

      I commence suit on a number of notes belonging to
your Husband estate before the war commenced Nothing has been done the break-
ing out of the war but now I suppose the courts will be held regualrly and
I wish to prosecute the suit most all my papers notes & c were destroyed
and I will be obliged to you if you will send me a copy of the receipt you
have of mine for the notes placed in my hand for collections. I have copies
of all the notes so that nothing will be lost I will have to only have to
swear to the amount of ech note which I can easily do as I took the precaution to take copies I wish th e copy of my receipt to compare with my copies
and see if there are any notes that I havent copies ofLet me hear from you
at your earliest convenience.

                Respectfully & C
                L. H. Bostick

RECORDS OF MRS. LULA ALGOOD (CON)

State of Tennessee No 2886
    To all to whom These Presents shall come, Greetings:
    Know ye, That for and in consideration of the sum of twelve and one half
cents per acre paid in the office of the Entry Taker of Overton County and
entered On the 29th day of June 1824 pursuant to provisions of an Act of the
General Assembly of saidState Passed on the twenty second day of Novemner,
one thousand eigth hundred and twenty three by No 166 there is granted by
the said State of Tennessee unto Nathan Bartlett A certain tract or parcel of
Land containing fifty acres by survey bearing date the 23 day of July/1825
lying in said county on both siades of the road leaving from William Marchbanks to Ann Quarles and bounded as followsto wit: Beginning at hickory at h
the foot of a mountain running South 23 d East with the mountain forty poles
to a post oak Thence South 40 Eadt with the mountain forty poles to a post
oak Thence with one hubdred and twenty six poles to aStake in a glade thence
N. Eighty two poles to a Stake and two black Jack pointers Thence East eighty four poles to a small white oak and chestnut pointer tyence South fifty
poles to the Beginning
    With the hereditaments and appurtenances To have an to hold the said
tract or parcel of land with its appurtenances to the said Nathan Bartlett
In witness whereof William Carroll, Govnor of the State of Tennessee, hath
hereunto set his hand and causednthe Great S al of the State to be affixed
at Murfreesborough on the Seventeenth day of November in the Year of Our
Lord one thousand eight hundred and twenty five and of the Independance of
Undted States the fiftieth

                              By Governor
                                 Daniel Graham
                                 Secretary
                        Wm Carroll

No 2886
Nathan Bartlett 50 acres
Overton County

Entry: John W. Simpson, Three hundred acres of Land in Jackson County on the Waters of Indian Creek (Caney Fork) Beginning on David M Clinttooks South West corner running North to Drapers line West so far as to include three hundred acres by adjoining Holemanslines, and the lines of two Entries ofself and with Holemans line to the beginning for complainant.

July 22nd, 1821 $300.John W. Simpson

No 966   A Copy O. R. Serenland, E. T. J. O.

No 966   John W. Simpson copy Entry 300 acres.

Entry: No 3040, made in office White County, entered Nov, 18, 1847Taken of White County entered Nov, 1837, granted by the State, 9, 1830, unto Isaac A.Huddleston , containing 68 acres surveyed Nov, 24, 1838on Waters of Little Caney Fork, Beginning, Pointer, Charles Huddleston South W. corner of 100 acressurvey, running then E. to John Bullock corner, then S, to BullecksS. West Corner, East then S. to Lewis Huddleston corner, thenW, then North, with a tract 300 acre That Isaac L Huddleston now liveson them run in Davis Huddleston line of 86 acre tract.

Test,   James K. Polk, Govner, of Tennessee,at Nashville,Tenn
                    Oct. 16, 1839.

                         By the Govner,
                              James K. Polk

Luke Lea, Secretary,

            Property of L. M. Bullington, Cookeville, Tenn, Putnam Co.

Deed: From David Huddleston to Isaac A. Huddleston, Jackson County, Oct, 17, 1850

     Consideration 106,00, District No 10, 100 acres, Beginning on the Co line Countys of Jackson and White, running South to Thomas Hopkins North b line, West North then South.

                              Daivid Huddleston (x his mark)

Tests   J. L. Huddleston,   Russell Moore, Clerk, Putnam County Court
         John L. Huddleston
         Ack, Sept 25, 1854,

Recd for Reg. Oct, 5, 1854, In Book A Page 35

                              William Baker,Reg,of Putnam County.

Reg. fee $1.00

State Tax 2 acres 15

            Property Of L. M. Bullington, Cookeville, Tenn. Putnam County

State Tennessee No 6931,Consideration one cent per acre paid in to office of the entry taker of Jackson County and entered May, 6, 1826, General Assembly of State passed on the 22 Nov.1823 and the acts Supplementalthereto, by No934 Granyed by the State Tennessee to David Huddleston Land 100acres, Dec. 15,1826 on Falling Water, bounded, Beginningat a Hickery on the County line dividing the counties of White andJackson, running with lineSouth. West, In Thomas Hopkins North boundry line West withHopkins line, then North then East, South to Beginning.

                    In witness whereof William Carroll, Govenor, of S. T.
                    Sealed at Nashville, Tenn, Sept. 25, 1827.
                         By Gov. Wm. Carroll
                         Daniel Graham, Secretary.

Reg. of D. McGavoc
    D. R.
Recorded Dec. 18, 1827
L. J. Summer,D. R.

The State of Tennessee No 7612
To all to whom these presents shall come, Greetings:
     Know ye that by virtue of certificate No 982 dated the 17th day of Aprile
1812 "esind" by the Register of West Tennessee to William P. Anderson and entered
on the 6 day of May 1812 by No 8090.
There is granted bt the said State of Tennessee unto David Young assigne of the
said WilliammP.Aderson a certain tract ofland cantaining two and a halfacres by
survey bearing date the 21 day of July 1813 lying in White County in the first
district on the Falling Water of Caney Fork and bounded as follows to wit:
Beginning at a White Oaksatandin about five poles below said Young lower salt
peterCave formelly worked by him running thende North twenty one poles to a post
on the side of a cleft thence West nineteen poles to a post and black gum chestnut & poplar pointers thence South crossing a hollow twenty one poles bytwo
hickorys thende east nineteen poles to the Beginning including said Young Cave.
With the Hereditoments & appartenances To have and to holdsaid tract or Parcel of
Land withits appurtenances to the said David Young and his heirs forever
In witness whereof
          Willie Blunt Govnor of the State of Tennessee Hath hereonto set his
hand and caused the great Seal of the State to be affixed at Nanhville on the
Nineteenth dayof Aug in the year of Our Lord one thousand eight hundred and fif-
teen and of the Independance of the United States the fortieth.
                              By the Govnor
                    W. G. Blunt,Secretary Willie Blont

David Young is entitled to the with in mentioned tract of land
                         D. M. Gavack Reg West Tennessee

Recorded in the Reg Office of West Tennessee, Sept 13, 1815
                         DM Gavack Reg.

No 7612 David Young
   2½ acres, White County.

State of Tennessee, Putnam County.

Personally appeared before me County Court Josiah Cole as describing to the with in deed of conveyance who being first sworn depose and say that he w was acquainted with the bargainers of the with in deed of conveyanceand that they acknowledge the same in his presenceto be their act and deed forthe purpose and things therein contained.

Witness my hand at office the 10th day of August A. D. 1857

Russell Moore, Clerk

State of Tennessee , Russell Moore, Clerk of Putnam CountyCourt John Jared as ascribing witness to the with in deed of conveyance who being first sworn depose and say thathe was acquainted with the bargainers of the with due deeds of conveyance and that they acknowledge the same in his presence to be their act andd deed for the purpose and things therein contained.

Witness myhand at the office th 14th day of December 1857.

Russell Moore, Clerk.

The following was written on the back of old deed)

The Annex Deed of conveyance was filed in my office and noted for registration in Reception Book Pages 56A57 on the 2nd day of January 1858 at 3 o'clock P. M. and regs in B. on Page 2, 13, 141 15, 16, and 17

William Baker, Register Putnam County.

Property of Virgil Denney Buffalo Valley, Tenn

Heirs of Mark Young, Dec. To Deed Distributive shares.
Clks. 50
State Tax 26.
Recorded on Page 147, Book A Putnam County, Tennessee,
R. Moore Clerk.

Clerk fee and Tax   76
Reg. fee   1.62½
Said to J. Anderson, State of Tennessee, Putnam County.
            To Moses Jared Esq. You are here by artherised and Empowered
to the examination of Leaner McKee, polly Ballard and Ruth Helens the fenal covet
Provately and apart from her husband relation to her free execution of the with
in or annaxed Deed and the same go taken certify ender your hand and witness.
            Russell Moore, Clerk of the County Court, Putnam County
at office the 15th day of Aprile A. D. 1857.
                        Russell Moore, Clerk, Putnam County.

Property of Judge F. Harris, Cookeville, Tennessee

STATE OF TENNESSEE, PUTNAM COUNTY.

I, E. H. Stone, Clerk of the County Court, do hereby certify that proof under Oath has been made before me that J. C. Freeze falls within the prevision of Section I, of an Act entitled "An Act to Limit the Elective Franchise" passed June 5th 1865, and is therefore a qualified voter of said County.

Given under my hand at office the 31 day of July, 1865.

E. H. Stone, Clerk.

C. N. C.   32

Dist. No 2

Gentlemen and Commissioners the undersigned wish you to employ Ralph Scott to Teh Teach the publick School at Nails School house We believe him to be competent as to Scholarship and he can give a good recommendation as a teacher July 16, 1848

No talking and laughin in time of School, no swaring, no climing cross no name incleur no telling tales in School nor out of School. No nicknaming-you must not go to no neighbors house at twelve oclock without make it none to meddelay no time going nor coming from school noquarling nor fiting .

All that is sixteen years old will quit School or take the licking if they brake the Rules.

(Contract for school teaching)

March 24th 1847

Mr. Monroe, Miller Brothers & Sisters,
Mr.& Mrs. Vandever request to your Company at the house on friday the 26th of this Inst. to a quiltin & N. B. You must come without fail;

I am Respectfully
WM M?Dawson

Mr. J. M. Miller
S Vally
Trd by Mr. Fergerson

Montgomery County, I do hereby certify that Robert Miller hath taken and subscribed the oath of affirmation of allegiance and fudelity, as directed by an act of General Affembly intituled An act to oblige the free male inhabitants of this ftate above a certain age to give afferance of allegiance to the fame and for other purposes, witness my hand seal this Death dn of Sept 1777.

Stephen Trigg   (Seal)

State of Tennessee, Putnam County : To any Regular Ordained Minister of the Gospel having the care of Souls or to any Justice of the Peace in and for said County ty or to any Judge or Chancler of said state Bond and security having bin given according to Law you are here but given or authorized to solemnize the Rites of Matrimony between Lancaster Randolf and Rebecca Shirley of said county and join them together as Husband and wife in the Holy Wedlock given under my hand at office this 27 day of November A. D. 1854

Russell Moore, Clerk
Putnam County Court.
by byrum C. Johnson,
Depty

Lancaster Randolf
    us   writ

Rebecca Shirley

Tax Receipts

June 30th 1813, Recd of Samuel Miller one dollar Seventy five cts in full of all amount against him Recd by me John Cain for
Samuel Harrison

Received this 28th Aprile 1817$ *15 cts from Samuel Miller fee direct tax upon the property of said Miller in the County of Overton, fer 1816 under the act of Congress foe the 3rd collective district of Tennessee.
    Under the act of Congress for the 3rd Collective District of Tennessee.

W. Brown, Dept
Collector 3rd District Tennessee

Cookeville, Tenn (Con)

Article made and Entered into We the Undersigned doth agree to imploy
James M. Miller To Teach School at the Stamps School house forthe Term of two
months said Miller doth agree to Teach the School to the best of his Skill and
Judgment at Eighty Cents per Schollar per month We the undersigned doth agree
to pay said Miller good Trade at the Market price such as young cattle or
pork hogsdelivered on foot or corn paid at the experation of the School this the 30
day of Sept, 1850

Name	Paid	
James Whiteaker	Paid	X
Mary Notherton	"	2
Joseph Henry	"	2
Job M. Jackson	"	2
William Stamps	"	3
James Stamps	"	X
John Henry	"	X X
Robert Roberts	"	X
Ldgeard Henry	"	X
Thomas Hill	"	X

(This Record is 165 Years Old)

This are to Certify that Robert Miller and His wife and her from her Childhood
up and him since he came amongst us the Both always Behaving them selves in a
Christian manner and may be Remembered to any Christian society where God
and his Providence shall order their lot Certified by us his day of May 15th
1771

Cedar Bridge Congregation,   J. L. River
                              James Gilmore
                              JohnPage

No. 12217

Department of the Interior

War of 1812   Survivors Pension

T. Certify That in Conformity with the Law of the United States approved February 14, 1871, Samuel Miller late a Lieutenant of Captain Jhos. Miller's Company Tenn Militia is inscribed on the Pension List Roll of the Nashville Tenn Agency at the rate of eight dollars per month to commence on the fourteenth day of February one thousand eight hundred and seventy one No Sale transfer or mortgage of any description whatever of the whole or any part of the pension payable in virtue of this certificate is of any legal or binding force against either the pensioner or the United States.

Given at the Department of the Interior this 7th Day of February, one thousand eight hundred and seventy two

B. O. Cowen

Actg Secertary of the Pensener

Examinined and Countersigned:

J. W. Batton

Commissioners of Pensions

Payable quarterly on the 4th of September and 4th of December at Nashville, Tenn

By William J. Stokes

U. S. Pension Agt.

John Mayhew Clerk

Records owned by Mrs. John Howard,
207- Poquat St. Cookeville, Tenn.

39

State of Tennessee, Putnam County.

To any Ordained Minister of the Gospel having the care of Souls, or to any Justice of the Peace for said county, or to any Judge or Chancellor of said state
Bond and security having been given according to law youare hereby authorized to solemnize the Rites of Matrimony between John Randolf and Mary Randolph of said county and join them together as Husband and wife in Holy Wedlock.
Given under my hand at office in Cookeville the IIth day of Dec. A. D. 1855.

Russell Moore, Clerk
Putnam County Court.

By virtue of the above License I have this day Solemnized the Rites of Matrimony between the parties therein named, in the presence of respectable witness.
Given under my hand this the day 1855.

John M. Randolf
To Marriage License
Mary Randolf
IIth Dec. 1855

State of Tennessee ,Putnam County

This indenture made and Entered into this 15ht day of November One Thousand
and Eight hundred and forty four Between Noah Sherly of the one Calvin Eldridge of
the other part both of county and State afore said his the Sd Noah Sherly for and
in consideration of the sum of one hundred dollars inhand by the said Calvin
Eldridge the recipt whereof is hereby firmly acknowleds hath granted bargained and
sold and by these presents doth grant Bargained and sell alien convey and confirm unto the Sd Calvin Eldridge his heirs Executors Administrators or assigns and
from all and every other person Claiming or to claim a tract or parcel of land
containing fifty acres be the same mere or less situated lying and being in the
County of Putnam and State of Tennessee his Beginning on Samuel Johnson North Bound-
ing line of his fifty acre currey on a popler running thence North West to a
Spotted Oak or the side of a ridge thence West bto a Chestnut on yhe top of the
Bench Thence meandering the top of the Bench to hutsons South line This Conditional
line between the two tracts now owned by Calvin Eldridge thence to Hustons corner
thence fourteen poles to Hustons Corner running West fourteen poles to a white oak
 and Sugar tree thence South one hundred and nineteen poles to a poplar and a chestnu
on a hillside thence East to Samuel Johnstons corner of his fifty acre Survey passing
same to Beginning with all the singular heredetiments and appertuances to have and
to hold for the use and benefit of the Sd Calvin Eldridge signed and delivered
in the presents of us
Attest--James M. Tenessee, Wm, Sparks , Noah Sherly   X His mark

By virtue of part of Said warrent of Christiany Tally Enters 20 acres of land
in our 3rd District and County of Overton on the Drye fork of oboe river
adjoining john Millers 50 acres Entry beginning at a black gum tree thence east
40 poles to a stake at the past of the bushey Mountain thence North 45 Deg. East
with said Mountain for complement

                    December 7th I809.
                        Christiany Tally
                            Locator

Christianys Tally's Location 20 acres.

The State of Tennessee, No 10143,

To all to whom these Presents Shall come Greetings: Know ye that in consideration of Military service performed by Benjamin C. Jeffries to the State of North Carolina Warrant No 4436 dated the 2nd day of Dec, 1796 and entered on the 15th day of November 1816 byNo 346 S, There is granted by said State of Tennessee unto Thomas Hopkins assignee of the heirs of the said Benjamin C Jeffries, a certain tract or parcel of land containing Thirty two acres part of Said Warrent by survey leaving date the 13th day of May 1815lying in White Countyin the third district on the waters the Falling Waters & East of the Wagon Road leading from Spark to William Jones Esq. and bounded as follows Towit: Beginning on two beeches near a marshy branch running thence South near the foot of the Mountain one hundred and two poles to aBeach & Dogwood, Thence Westfifty poles to a white oak near a branch , Thence North one hundred and two poles to three blackoaks, Thence East including Welches improvements to the Beginning. With the hereditaments and appurtenances, To have and to hold the said tract or parcel of land with its appurtenances to the said Thomas Hopkins and his heirs forever in witness whereof Joseph McMinn, Gov. of the State of Tennessee hath hereunto set his hand and caused the Great Seal of the State to be affixed at Knoxville on the Eleventh day of June in the Year of Our Lord one thousand eight hundred and seventeen and of the Independenac of the United States for the forty First.

By the Governor.

Wm. Alexander Secretary.   Joseph McMinn.

Recorded in the Registers office of West Tennessee, Sept.26th 1817

D. M. McGavock, Reg.

Property of Judge B. G. Huddleston, Cookeville, Tenn. Putnam Co.

State of Tennessee No 20516, To all to whom these Presents shallCome,Greetings: Know ye that virtue of a part ofcertificate No 2535 dated thol3thday of November1816 ipued by register of West Tennessee toRobert Searcy for 320 acres and entered on the 21st dayof March 1817 No 5369, There is granted by the State of Tennessee unto Charles Huddleston assignee of the said Robert Searcy, a certain tract or parcel of land containing Twelve acres by survey leaving date of 22 day of October 1818 lying in theThird District in White County on the waters of the Falling Waters and bounded as follows towit: Beginning at the South east corner of Welches 32 acre survey running thence east twenty four poles to a stake and pointers on the side of theMountain thence North along the same as a natural landing eighty poles to a pointers thence West striking said Huddlestons corner and with the same twenty four poles to Welches corner thence South along hisline eighty poles to the Beginning. With the hereditaments and appurtenances to have and to holdthe said tract or parcel of land with its appurtenances to the said Charles Huddleston and his heirs forever. In witness whereof William Carroll, Governor,of the State of Tennesseehath hereunto set his hand caused the Great Seal of the State to be affixed at Murfreesborough on the 25th day of September in the Year of Our Lord one thousand eight hundred and twenty three and of the Independance of the United States the forty eight.

Wm. Carroll. Gov.

Daniel Graham, Secretary

Property of Judge B. C. Huddleston, Cookeville, Tenn
Putnam County.

42

This Indenture made and entered into this fifth day of August in the Year of Our
Lord one thousandEight hundred and nenetsen between Thomas Ingram heirs and legal
representative of William Ingram,Decd. of the County of Hawkins and State of
Tennessee by William Mitchell his attorney in fact of the one part andCharley Huddleston and John C. Huddleston of the county of White and State afore said of
the other part, witnessoeth that for and in consideration of the sumeof two thous-
and dollars current money to him the said Thomas Ingram his legal representative
of William Ingram Decd. in land paid by the said Charles Huddleston & John C.Hud-
dleston the receiptwhereof he doth hereby acknowledge and thereof doth elquith
and power dischargethem the said Charles Huddleston and JohnC. Huddleston their
heirs executors and administrators , Doth Grant bargans sell aline enposaed and
confirmed unto them the said Charles Huddleston and Jihn C. Huddleston, their heirs
and assigns forever two certain tracts and parcel of land containing in allthree
hundred and forty acres lying and ening in the County of White and State of Tennessee to William Ingram by Grant No 13252 for 100 acres and Grant No 13253 for 200 a
acres Granted to the heirs of William Ingram, Decd., both dated the 1st day of Apr.
1819, and bounded as follows Towit: G ant No 13252 Beginning at two small hickory
the South West corner to Wolsey W. Pearses occupant survey running South and bounded forty poles to a stake thence East one hundred and sixty poles to a small white
oak and water white oak on the South side of ridge, thence North one hundred and
forty poles to a white walnut mulberry andelm and said Pearces South boundry, Thence
West with Pearces line one hundred and sixty poles to the Beginning including part
of the land originally surveys as an occupant right in the name of Joel Alexandria
Grant No 13253 for 200 acres bounded as followsTowit: Beginning at a stake thesouth
West Corner of William Ingram 140 acres boundry line thence East one hundred and
sixty poles to a white oak andwater white oak Wm. Ingram South East corner thence Sou
South two hundred poles to a black oak & twowhite oaks, thence West one hundred
and sixty poles to a stake a chestnut black oak & two post oak pointers near an at
road, thence North two hundred poles to theBeginning including part of the land
formerly surveyed as an occupant sight in the name of Joel Alexandria,Togather,
with the hereditaments and appurtenances, To have and hold the above tracts or
parcels of land to gather with the hereditaments and appurtenanc es thereunto or
in any wise assertaining to the only proper use of them the said Charles and Jno.
C. Huddleston their heirs and assigns forever, and the said Thomas Ingram heir and
legal representative of William Igram Decd. for himself his heirs, Executors
administrators and assigns the title interest claim and demand of in recd. to the
above discribed tracts or parcel of land will warrent and forever defend unto them
the said Charles Huddleston and John C. Huddleston their heirs, executorsadministra-
tors and assigns against the right title claim interest or demand of all and all
manner of person or personsclaiming or to claim the same or any part thereof,
In Testimony whereof be the said Thomas Ingram by his attorney in fact William
Mitchell hath hereunto set his hand and affixed his seal the day and year first above
written signed, sealed and Acknowledged in presence of,

     A. R. Low
     Rashford Irwin (Xhis mark)
     William Mitchell, all yenfail for
      Thomas Ingram

State of Tennessee, October session, A. D. 1819, W. County
  The due execution of the foregoing Deed of Conveyance from Thomas Ingram
to Charles Huddleston and John C. Huddleston was this day acknowledged in open
court by William Mitchell attorney in fact for Thomas Ingram for the payment
and things therein mentioned andordered to be recorded let be Registered Given
at office the 18th day of october, 1819.

     Jacob A Lane, Clerk (Seal)
     Putnam County Court by his Depty,
     A. R. Lane

Recd. the State Tenn,
Test of Conveyance,

State of Tennessee, White County, Thomas Barnes, Esq. comes before M. Samuel
Johnson an actingJustice of the Peace qr. said county and made oath that some-
timebetween the sixth & twentieth of June test that John Cleghorn andCharles
Huddleston come before him and confess three judgments on three notes for eighty five dollarsEighty seven 4¢ per cts each in favor of William Hunter sew which¢
notesa warrent was left by him the said Thomas Barnes in the handsofWilliam
Hows Esq. of Jackson County to render the judgment on eachwarrent which warrents
was to have been transferred by the said Wm.Hows, Esq. to him the said Thomas
Barnes on the day after residition of the said judgment which means was the said
Thomas Barnesfurther deposeth & Layeth the reason why he got William Esq. to
write the judgment for himwas that he had been after medicinefer his son who was v
very sick at that time & the parties following him to act on the notes a day
after they confessed judgmenton the notes both parties agreedthat hewas in a
hurry to get home that said William Hows should write the judgment agreed to
the amount ef the notes.

Sworn to & Subscribed to before me, Lamb Johnson, Justice of the Peace.
January ,11, 1821

Thos. Barnes,
Affidvit-

State of Tennessee, No 2039. To all to whom these presents shall come, Greetings—

Know ye that for and in consideration of sum of twelve and one half cents per acre paid into the office of the Entry Taker of Jackson County and entered on the 26th day of June 1824 pursuant to the provisions of an act of the General Assembly of said State passed on the 22nd day of November 1823, by No 144, there is granted by the State of Tenn. unto Charles Huddleston a certain tract or parcel of Land containing Fifty acres by survey bearing date the 2nd day of Aprile 1825, lying in the said county on the waters of the Falling Waters and bounded as follows, to-wit: Beginning a t a black oak it being rhe South corner of said 20 acre tract then East with North boundry line of said tract twenty poles to a hickory in Thomas Bernes West boundry line thence North said Barnes line forty five poles to a post oak the south east corner of said Huddlestons 15 acre tract thence west with the south boundry line of said 15 acre tract twenty four poles to a stake and two chestnut pointers, thence North thirty six poles to a Spanish oak the Norty west corner of sd said Huddleston 15 acre tract, thence West twentyseven and a half poles to a hickory thence South one hundred and twenty one poles to a Spanish oak, thence east forty one and one half poles to the beginning. With the hereditaments and appurtenances to have and to hold the said tract or parcel of land with its appurtenances to the said Huddleston and his heirs forever. In witness whereof William Carroll, Governor of the State of Tennessee hath hereunto set his hand and caused the Great Seal of the United States to be affixed at Murfreesborough on the 13th day of August in the Year of Our Lord one thousand eight hundred and twenty five and the Independance of the United States the fiftieth

                                  By the Governor, Wm. Carroll

Daniel Graham, Sec.
Recorded in the Registers office of West Tenn. Feb. 4th, 1826
                                  H. W. McGavock, D. R.

              Property of Judge B. C. Huddleston, Cookeville, Tenn Putnam Co.

State of Tennessee No 20511-To all to whom these presents shall come, Greeting:
Know ye that by virtue of part of Certificate No 943 dated the 2nd day of June 1815 ipued by the Register of East Tennessee to Nathaniel Taylor for 50 acres and entered on the 25 th day of August 1815 by No 4114, There is granted by the State of Tenn, unto Charles Huddleston assignee of the said Nathaniel Taylor, a certain trat or parcel of land containing fifteen acres by survey leaving date the 17th day of February 1816 lying in the Third District in White County on the waters of Falling Waters and bounded as follows to wit: Beginning at a hickory and white oak on the W West boundry line of Thomas Barnes claim and near the foot of the Mountain running thence east sixty nine poles to a chestnut and postoak on said Barnes line thence North to the Beginning. With the hereditamenst and appurtenances to have and to hold the said tract or parcel of land with its Appurtenances to the said Charles Huddleston and his heirs forever, In witness whereof William Carrolle, Gov. of the State of Tennessee hath hereunto set his hand and caused the Great Seal of the State to be affixed at Murfreesborough on the 25th day of September in the Year of Our Lord one thousand eight hundred and twenty three and the Independance of the United States the forty eight.

                                  By the Governor, William Carroll.
                                  Danile Graham, Secretary.

State of Tennessee, White County, I, Turner Lane , Register of the County of White
of aforesaid Do hereby certify that the within Deed of Conveyance together with the
testimonies thence endorsed was this 15th day of December, A. D. 1819 Registered
in the register's office of said county fo White in Book F. and Page 374 given
under my hand at office the date above written.

Test-   Turner Lane, Register
   Thos. Ingram   To 340 acres in 2 tracts.
   Shas. & Thos. C. Huddleston

          Property of Judge B. C. HUddleston, Cookeville, Tenn,

   I, Charles Huddleston have this day bargaor and sold and do hereby Transfer &
convey to Jordan F. Huddleston his heirs& assigns forever for the consideration of
Fifty Dollars to one in hand paid a certain Tract or Parcel ofland in the State of
Tennessee, Putnam Co, District No1 containing by estimation Eighteen and a half
of acres be the same more or less and bounded as follows,Beginning on a mountain
oak the said Jordan F. Huddleston South East corner running South 40 poles to a
stake &pointers the South East corner A 12 acres Grant No 20516 Granted to the said
Charles Huddleston thence West 74 poles to a white oak near a small branch, thence
North 40 poles to a stake & Dogwood pointerthe said Jordan F. Huddleston South E.
corner, Thence East 74 poles to the beginning to have and to hold the same unto
the saidJordan F. Huddleston his heirs & assigns forever I do covenant with the
said Jordan F. Huddleston That I am Lawfully seized of said land have a goodright
to convey it and thatthe same unencumbered I dothen covenant and bind myself my
heirs and Representatives to warrant and forever defendthis title to the said land
   and Every part thereof to the said Jordan F. Huddleston South East corner, Thence
East 4 poles tothe beginning to have and to hold the same unto the said Jordan F.
Huddleston, his heirs & assigns forever. I do covenant with the said Jordan F. Huddleston That I am Lawfully seized of said land have good right to convey it and
That the same is unencumbered I do for this covenant and bind myself, my heirs &
representatives to warrent and foever defend land and every part there to the said
Jordan F. Huddleston his heirs & assigns against the lawful claims of all persons
whatsoever this 26th day of January, A. D. 1839,

                                       Charles Huddleston (Seal)

Test-Russell Moore
    Joe Algood

State of Tennessee, Putnam County, Personally appeared before me Russell Moore, Clk.
of Putnam County Court Charles Huddleston the within bargainer with whom I am
personally acquainted and who acknowledge the due execution of the within deed of
conveyance to be his act and deed for the purpose andthings therein contained is
Recorded witnessed my hand at office the 26 day of January, 18 39

                                       Russell Moore, Clerk
The written deed of conveyance was filed for Registration on the 26th day of Jan.
1839 & was noted on filation Book at pages 84& 85 at 4 p. m. I was registered on
Book C. pages 181& 182

                                       S. W. Brown, Reg.

Charles Huddleston To Deed 18½ acres
    Jordan F. Huddleston State Tax
    Clerk Fee 25
Reg.   Fee   105 Paid.

State of Tennessee No 7743-

To all to whom these presents shall come, Greetings, Know ye that by virtue of E
Entry No 2517 made in the office of the Entry Taker of Jackson County and entered
on the 4th day of December 1837 pursuant to the provisions of an act of General
Assembly of said State passed on the 9th day of January 1830, There is granted by
the said State of Tennessee unto Chas. Huddleston a certain tract or parcel of
Land containing Eighteen acres and Eighteen poles by survey bears date the 27th
day of November 1838 situated in said County Beginning at a small Spanish Oak and
past Oak and Spanish Oak and past Oak pointer the South East corner of a fifty
acre survey that the said Huddleston now lives on running thence West with the Sou
South boundry line of said survey forty and one half poles to two Spanish oaks the
SouthWest corner of said fifty acres survey thence North with the West boundry
line of said survey one hundred and twenty one poles to a hickory which is now
dead four dogwoods and black gum pointers the North West corner of said fifty
acre survey, Thence West and xix and one half poles to a small hickory and hickory and dogwood pointers in the E. Boundry line of an old survey Granted to Wm.
Ingram thence South with the E. boundry line of the same an hundred and sixty five
poles to a white oak and pointers in the North boundry line of David Huddleston one
hundred acre tract thence E. with the North boundry line of the same forty eight
poles to a stake in the West boundry line of a thirty two acre tract, now belonging to the said Chas. Huddleston, thence North forty four poles. With the
Hereditaments and appurtenances to have and to hold the said tract or parcel of
land with its appurtenances to the said Chas. Huddleston and his heirs forever.

      In witness where of James K. Polk, Gov. of the State of Tennessee has
hereto set his hand and caused the Great Seal of the State to be affixed at
Nashville on the 9th day of December 1839, C. 4th year of an Independance.

                                   By the Governor,
                                   James K/ Polk.

Jno. S. Young, Secretary.
Charles Huddleston is entitle to the within described tract of land
                              Richard Nelson, Reg.of the Mountain Dis.

                              By W. G. Sims D, register
Recorded in my office Book P. Page 325
                              R. Nelson, Regst. of the Mountain Dist.

No 7743   Charles Huddleston, 18 acres and 18 poles, Jackson County.
Filed for registration in my office February 6th, 1855, at 10 o'clock a. m.
Registered in Book A-and Page 132-133&134
                              William Baker, Reg. for Putnam County
11 state------$2\frac{3}{4}$

(From Collection of Mrs. B. C. Huddleston, Cookeville, Tenn. Putnam Co)

LIVINGSTON COUNTY MISSOURI,
JULY 14, 1845.

My Dear Father & Mother, Brothers & Sisters:

God bears me witness when I say that I know not how to begin to write
to you, not-with-standing I am young yet I have wrote several letters, But this
Cadmus, I was taught from my child-hood not when I say that thou wert a false
prophet, yea, I say that htou wert a fool: If thou ever thought that thy flimsey
invention though multiplied in to forty thousand ways, would be a full conduc-
tor to a Father & Mother of the feelings and emotionsof an absent child, as this
is worthless then I command the not but ask the to touch their hearts Almighty
with the remembrance of by gonedays. Wake up; O,thou muse of other times and seasons, Bring flesh to some of their memory's the feelings of their own hearts,
Almighty, with the remembrance of bygone days, Wake up O thou muse of other times
and seasons, Bring flesh to some of hteir memory's the feelings of their own hearts
on the 12th of Aprile, 1810, and the first of Aprile 1812, that they may the bette
know the felings of their own child on the day of the first cause of this epistle
the 11th of Aprile, 1845.

Mother, though the long lapse of thirty two years has passes I doubt not
but you will recall your mother's valedictions on the12th of Aprile 1812. Little
did you then think you would see her no more on earth Hard sorrowful it is to
part with friends, but it is harder still to part with her on whose bosom in
helpless infancy we slept and from whose benevolent veins we draweth the first
supportof life. There is something in it which the painters brush has never touchd
and the writers pen has never told, But it is so, From the mammoth to the mite,
that can't be caught by microscopic eye neither and I loath to say it was so with
me, For I know no man on earth ever loved his Father more than I love mine or more
tnan I on every one of his brothers and Sisters wished a greater Blessing than
on himself, Yet I say that it hurts me worse than all the rest to part with thee-
and though into an unutterably full and thankful heart I received al l their
prayers and last words and remembered them well-yet thine I shall never forget.
For oft that day as the roaring of theStage wheels died away in echoon the dest-
ant hills, I could see thy venerable form drawn with thediseases and afflictions
of the body and sorrows of mind, as thouraised thy withered hand and in agonizing
prophetic tones that sounded like a death knell to my heart. The agonizing prophetic tones that sounded like a death knell to my heart, exclaimed I shall never
no never, see my Child again.

O, my God, the agony of that moment, a prophecy concerning another one
of thy children and now an unknown grave in a distant land interperts the prophecy
Will mine be so Oh God, Thou knowest.

The sun was two hours high when we arrived at Carthage. The other Stage
came not till dark and as the general confusion of the city and land laughs of the
young men just returning from muster, did not corrospond with my feelings, I tooka
walk through the back streets andold lanes until I found myself upon the banks of
the river. I satdown upon the green grass to my wonted employment a long and silent
meditation, Up the river in full view was the confluence of the Caney Fork and
Cumberland. I was looking at the immediate waters of my native land perhaps for th
the last time and as I strained my eyes far up the clear blue waters of the forme
I imagined I could see its very fountains bursting out from beneath the mountain
bas, I could see the sweetest ofearths fountains where first I water uses knew,
where oft in childhoods happy hours I slaked my burning thirst and cooled my
heated brow. Then, too, I could see my noble old grand fathers where I have spent
many happy hours in my childhood wandering its melancholy way around the deserted
dwellings and lonesome orchard of thet oncebhappy place, Neither did I ever look
one that runs from beneath thegrove where my own Father lived and where I had

spent my later years.

Then, too, where the waters of the pleasant grove where from the score of saints ascended prayers for me when a disconsolated mourner, there is imagention I could see them all as on there gravelly beds they went gently murmering down, mingling joining in one as if to showpoor vain selfish hearted man, that united thet could carry their course even amid the mighty hills and barriers and that he himself, by devisions, wrangling and quarreling was proving the death of that heaven born truth, he trying to establish.

Many were the reflections I had at this place, Many the thoughts of days that are gone. Alas, gone forever. So great is the nature of the Soul that a volume is but a preface to what I thought and felt in that hour. Loud would I ask myself"If you be a land of such tall groves, sweet sorings and heaven inspieing breezes, Why do I have to leave thee? Why go from my father and Mother , Brothers and Sisters , Friends? Yea, all I have ever knew and all that was ever dear to me? Who have I murdered? Whose goods have I stolen? What great eveil have I done that I mustexile myself from them forever? Has slander with her hateful poisonous tongue tried to disgrace me with the family to whom I allow it an honor to belong? Do I go forth like Cain leaving my Father's family weeping more for my crimes than the loss of hteir Brother out of their circle? To none of these questions would my heart respond, Yea and I was lost as to what was the cause, Amid a thousand perplexing and unsatisfactory conjectures: "O thou, I exclaimed" who fixed the destiny ofman, who directeth the paths of hisfeet and pondereth all his goings Thou who directed with the samecare the fate of nations and heroes and causeth the blood in the veins of the fly, Tell me, Show me the cause Alas? I implore in vain,"I seem to be unobserved by God and all his creatures until evercome with anguish of Spirit my head insensibly sank upon my knees and I gave way to a relieving flood of tears, when I raised my eyes it was growing dusk, a blue mist was upon the waters, A spestre arosefrom the stream with seven large letters, him name, Written on his brow, O, could you have seenthat Spirit you would not blame me for writing a lengthly about him. His pale solem melancholy look; his tattered raiment, hisanxious deep gazing countenance. The heart of the affluent stoic though made of steel would have shed a tear over his forlorncondition. The dregs of disease were seated in his vitals whishtime and circumstances had changed into that most loathsome of all diseases, Dyspepsia. His cou tenance that was once happy and cheerful was notovercast with despondence and gloom and as I very anxiously gazed upon it my eye caught the letter on his brow; Hah "Poverty" I exclaimed and hevanished from my sight. The vision was of a moment and theinterpretation was of the same , and it is the Thou Unhappy fiend thatconducteth my hence Yea I see it, I feel it; I know it now. O, poverty; unfortunate, unhappy , unwelcome guest how many sweet daughters hast thou torn from a mothers heart and sent them into a land of strangers to fine a sustenance wherelieu they soon found an earlygrave? How many sons hastthou raised up and thrust out from their fathers to the utt ernost parts of the earth to make a fortune and a home and then threwpoor poor worm give up the ghost and die and know not wheather heleaves themt to a wise man or a fool? Yea, Time and Fate and circumstances has decreed it so fm from the foundation of the Earth Go to the Land of Nod and ask Cain and he will tell thee it was so with him and as thou returnest the Sons of Europe, Asia and Africa willc ry out unto thee: It was so with our Fathers "Yea the voice of Jacob hears witness to what I saw as he lay alone in the gloom of plains of Padan-Aran and it is answered by a sigh from the youthful Jacob aspensively he sat in the dark walls of Potiphars prison. Then, O, Thou director of all things as thou hast decreed it so with me I go resigned. I was stopped short in the midst of my meditations by the shrill sound of the drivers horn which told me the other stage had arrived. I arosefrom the ground, twas growing dark and pointing my hand up the stream exclaimed, "Tennessee; Land of my friends, Lands of my Fathers, Thou only place I ever loved, thou only place I ever knew, Farewell, Blow on Heavenly breezes, Blow on and you tall nuciferous groves bend your giant heads and mingle yu youth linesome praise with theirs for ages yet to come,And you that first attracted my mindsoyr , your crystal fountain of my Fathers Farewell— and should I ever

(From Collection of Mrs. B. C. Huddleston ConO)

taste thy cooling waters more continue to pore out thy jasper treasures, Flow a
down the vale untill like thy formerowners and their children thou art scattered and lost in Times mightydispersion, And thou nearestone to the place of
meditation like the old Spring of Castalia, may youpertify your attendants in
righteousness, that as they meet from year to year to celebrate the works of
the Lord they may continue teoffer up prayers for me for I am a mourner yet
and will be to my grave For my heart is in the house of mourning but the heart &
of the fool is in the house of mirth, (Ecs.7, 4) Come to me thou narrow hearted
selfconceited sectarian and look at one who has the satisfying pleasure of feeling the same love for all the laborers in God's vine yard yes go the same Method-
ists, the Indolent Denominations, I point the to them for the same purpose
that Solomon pointed the sluggard to the ant , Thou Pleasant Grove Fountain Field
Wood, and Friends, Farewell. And should I never again in body be with thee, oft
in summer evenings twilight gray thou mayst see me in your mind eye as through
your fileds I pass in the Golden Balloon Of Imagination, In a few Moments.

In a few moments we were sailing down the road towards old man dusk. We
entered Nashville. We were up late that night. The next evening at business.
Next morning at 8 O'clock when we got our matters finished, I went to the
office to get Spartan's letter and drop Bro. Watson a line. The letter was not
there although ithas since come by mail. I hurried back tomthe river, when I
arrived the boat was unmoored. I sprang aboard and in twentyfour hours I was in
Smithland. Here we waited twenty hours for a boat passing from Pittsburg to St.
Louis and on Tuesday morning the 15th at sunrise we embarked on an Orleans boatt
come from the South. As I stood here watching the slow blue waters of Ohio as
they gently flow and poured into the Indians "Mad waters" and wasrapidly hurried
off to the burning plains of the South. I could but exclaim with the Old Prophet
I am a Hebrew and I fear the Lord , the God of Heave, that made the sea and
the dry land. At 2 o'clock a boat from Orleans stopped . We embarked and on Thu
rsday morning the 17th we hove in sight of the glittering spires of St.Louis.
There was near thirty boats anchored here and soon as we landed we hurried up
the wharf watching the signsuntill we found that read Black Snake Hills, 4
o'clock this day" We went to the Captain made the arrangements, put our things
aboard and having nine hours to stay we set out to search for Dorinda's grave.
We went to the house where she died and consulted with Houston as the best
means to proceed. He advised us to go to a place called Black Stables as the
Sexton had lived there. We went there. They could tell us nothing of the sexton
and his name was not on the Books. They directed us to the Catholic Cathedral
Wewentthere and old Father Panco could'ntfind her name on his books. He directed
us to the city Register. We went there and her name could not be found , not
with standing there were numbers of graves in and around the place, and we knew
not to which one to go. We determined to go no more of the register and we set
out to hunt till we found it. Between 10 and 11 o'clock we found the grave yard.
Although twas dark when he was there before, he knew the place and showed me
where the carrage came in. There is about six acres enclosed, embracing two
largesinks and a sharp ridge between, we followed the road around on the ridge
till we came to the place where the hearse stopped.Now we knew we were in ten
feet of her grave. Mother, shed not a tear when I tell you that though I was now
so I could put my handon her grave(I wanted to have it walled in if it had
taken mt lastgroat) but we could not tell which it was. We stayed there an
hour or more, the sexton with us trying to ascertain but no purpose. I shall not
attempt to say anything about my feeling as I turned and left the grave. Sleep
on, My Sister, Sleep on. Though our bodies are close together theyknow it not
our Spirits arecloser still and though thy wasted frame lies here

Amid a land of Strangers
Alone unepitaphed, unshrouded, Enregistered , unknown,

FROM COLLECTION OF MRS. B. C. HUDDLESTON (CON)

Ifthyy nemm is not registered here it is in Heaven,
By Angels hands
Whose pen is quill from his rthereal wing,
And his ink is liquid gold,
Whereby the Telescope of Faith I see thee now,
Looking on the family record
Anxiously waiting to see the only remaining
Two enrolled.
I could write a volum on this half would'nt then be told
But I leave it in the hands as the Poet did his case,
When he felt all and had no words to express it he said
" Come, thou expressive Silence, Tell the tale"
     We left St. Louis at sunset Friday 18th and Tuesday night at dark the 22
we reached Brunswick and on the morning of the 23rd we struck into the
PrairiesI felt as the Israelites must have felt when they saw all the beau-
ties of the Old Jewish Caanan. There was now befoer my mortal eyes a most
pleasing prospect a more delightful view than I had ever pictured even in
my Imagirtion. For thirty miles, Yea farther then the eye could see twas an
uninterrupted sea of waving grass without the entervention of a tree or shn
shrub on Tuesday morning we reached my brother in laws and found them all
well and getting on finely in the world. I reckon there was joy at our arrival. Many were the questions about you all and many the answers, forgetting
the pwtty faults and turning them into graces.
     In a day or two I went on to Ruben Perkins and nothing would do now but I
must teach them a school. He had been looking for me out here for months and
had determined that as soon as I came I should teach them a school. I told
them that in ten days I was going on to G$_o$shen and from there to Platte and
that I should not be here again for months.
     Louisa would'nt listen to me talking of setting anywhere only close to hr
and we kept on till finally I told him if he would make me up a school if
my breast would permit I would teach them a school for six months.
     On the 11th day of May I went to Gishen. I found all well there, met my
Aunt Nancy, Old man McClelland, Ruben and Maria a mile or two this side of
Uncle Rhea's. Mother, My Aunt is the most hale healthy looking woman you evr
saw. I rode with her that evening home and ask her the cause of such an un-
common change in her health and person she told me it was the air. She said
said when she first came here she thought she had never felt such a delightf-
ful breezein her life and she would go out in the yard to a flat rail she
had and get on the top of the fence and let the wind blow on her for hours
and this is what brought her to. It would take a fence indeed to hold her now
So much for the breeze of Missouri. At two hours by sun we arrived at her
house an excellent ferm. They are getting rich. The children are all much
improved. The next day the 12th we went to Brother John McClellends Iwish I
had room to tell you something about how he is fixed. If you could see it
you would not blame him for not wanting to go back to Tennessee to live.
     Thursday the 13th I went to L--- to see old man Linsey and if I had been
John it seemed they could not have been much better pleased to have me. I
reached their house about 2 o'clock and stayed till 10 o'clock the next day.
The old lady and me went ot the kitchen and talked a hmng time time I talked
to her just as if she had been my own mother without any hems and haws about
it. I told her it was the general impression in Tennessee

that they wanted to go back. How the boys had been talking of coming after them and that they had relenquished the idea for this reason., simply that I could find out as much as them and let them know. She was hurt at your havingfailed to move and more particularly at your not coming to look at th country. "Tell J hn, said she If he ever lives with me it will be here for I know I shall never got to Tennessee again" The next morning I left there and turned toward Goshen and dined with Kizzie Ray. You don't know how glad she was to see me. The day my cousin Susna and me went up to see Miranda. I had a fine time with them all, of which I will tell uoi more, Loga when I write to you for I am going to write to you and Amos and Dan and other of the neighbor boys that ought by all means be here. You know Logan? I did not expect to like this country but I say so far as I know now I am well pleased with it When I returned from Goshen Ruben Perkins had my school mad mad up. Two months of the six are gone and I am clearing $1.04 per day. I have an excellent claim between brother Johns and my school house, at which work evenings and on Saturdays. I have another across the Creek with an excellent spring on it anda large shingle roof house which there seems to be no owner, though oneman claims it and says he will take ten dollars for his claim. I am going to buy it the first time I see him and then I wi will have an excellent place forsome of my friends. Mother, My school house is a large hewed log house with a excellent plank floor. It is our church. There was singing at it last Sunday was week and old Brother Thompson preached a sermon there yesterday, one today and will preach another this evening. The clerk of the Court is down and waiting for my letter to take to the office.

Farewell,
C. W. to R. F. and Margaret Cook.

Iwrote my letter a week ago and have waited a week to hear from Goshen. There are four coming down from there to go to school. I looked for them this evening, but can't wait for the news they bring. Aunt and Uncle Rhea was down a week ago, all was well and Bro John trying to make him a school. Don't know how it resulted.

Don't fail to send my books by Jim Whitefield. All the friends send love to you, Betsy Perkins in particular.

(Calvin Whitley Cook was born Mar, 18, 1825, so was twenty years old when this letter was written. The date 1810 refers to the time of their , his father and mother leaving Virginia to come to Tennessee.)

LETTER TO COL. SEBIRD RHEA FROM RICHARD C. M. COOK.
OWNED BY MRS. B. C. HUDDLESTON? COOKEVILLE? TENN.

Double Springs, June 5th,
Jackson, County, Tenn.

Monday Morning, June 5th, 1848,
Dear Bro. & Sister—

I received your favor of the 10th of Aprile By the Hand of Johns Louisa Perkins vivi at my house on the 15th of Maywith out any accident & all well, you may Judge, But we cannot express our joy— they found us all in usual helth and have visited many of their friends and old acquaintances and are gone to see Harriet. She was married last fall to Willaim Oscar Howe and lives near the white plains he is a young man of fine appearance & good sense & has a good start in the world Your sisters Byers & Family with other friends in general are well— I have had accounts from Brother John William Alexan and Elias this spring all well— Bro. John wrote that Sister Sallie Goodgains with several of her family was gone to Texas to live he persuaded her to continue with him but she chose to go with her children which was natural to expect. We shall seeher no more, though as a family we have been blest with general helth and has by the help of God Been permitted to continue almost unbroken to a good old age— though death has spared most of us, yet it has fell to my lot to pass through and other trying since somt time before Christmas last our Brother Jess a Cook was attacked with something like Typhus fever and on the 5th day of January he departed this life and I buried him by the sister of our Father. He was willing to go, all is well I much Regretted to hear of Spartians affliction which had been of so long a continuance and of so serious a character though I still hope he may Recover as Bird C. Kinslow once lay near five months in a semlar condition & contrary to all Expectation finally recovered. I am much pleased to hear that your selves and your children are all doing well I should bemuch gratified were it in my power to see you all though I begin to Doubt ever havong that pleasure, as I find age advancing a pace and wi with it an increase of flesh and the loss of action, Incident to those who have past three score years. it is time to cast our eyes down toward the tomb instead of look to the world for its good or Hapiness our family are all gone and we are left alone thiugh blest with usual helth & plenty I find myself denied that Tranquility of mind I am antisipated after seeing all our children raised and Educated and able to provide for themselves. Yet I have as little cause of complaint as otherswho have been bereft of children in all ages of the world. My son Watson who is here doing well & has made a man Equal to my most sanguin wishes But our other two are gone & whereon to Organ & the other to the Mexican war perhaps to see them no more, which may heaven forbid, But we are human & hear our pray thiugh God is able to save that which seems to be lost I will therefor hope We feel grateful for your kind attentions to our Request in Regard to your Enquery afterWhitley which I wish you to continue to do By every opertunity that you think you have any chance to hear from him and By way of Rewarding your faithful attentions to my Request I must inform you that I take the Earliest opertunity of informing youthat on last Sunday we had the Joy of Receiving a letter from him Bearing date the23 Day of Dec. last he was in Organ, but Every sweet has its bitter, he informs that the Indians has broke out and killed and destroyed a Missionary Station in the Walla Walla Vally and he was on the poit of Statging as a voluntier against them there is four tribes that has beeen host and the Emigrants has sent Wm. Meeks to the City of Washington to obtain assistance from the goverment though I am at a loss to see how troops can be got there in time to save the Colony. Mr. Meeks Brought the latter to St Joseph & then it was mailed I shall write in hopes of his Return soon from Washington & that he

will convey it on the City of organ ,Whitley is well pleased with the country
and says if he lives he will Return in 1849. I have seen Meeks Journal in the
papers and he states that they had had four engagements with the Indians
before he got out of the Territory in all of whichthe whites had been Successful he left the army only four hindred strong on the 26th of January & the
first Battle was fought on the 8th of the same month, two weeks after Whit-
leys letter was Rote I will also Inform you that the letter last Bolivor &
Col. John Seartland Raised a voluntear company in going through and about th
17th Statted to Mexice Seartland command the company and Bolivor is Lieutenant, they landed at Veniarys about the 20th of November and passed immediat-
ly on to the City of Mexico, where they have continued the most of the winter.

        Seartland was taken sick soon after they got there and the command
Divolved on Bolivor Everlense I Received a letter from Seartland the other dy
day, he informed me that he would join his company again in a Day or two.
Boliver haswrote many letters to us his health has been good and if peace
is made Rite he will be home soon if he lives, if peace is not made he will
not come till next Aprile.

        We were at preaching last Sunday at Masidonia on Cane Creek and there
saw a great many of your old relatives & friends among them Wm P. Peak, A.
Ditty, Campbells cous Ellison & all as far as I heard in usual health. Sam-
uail Rays funeral was pneached by William Townsden and a great many people
out, I wish you to never cease Riting to us as long as you can see to make
a letter and now farewell.

                    S. & Nancy Rhea-Richard F. C. M. Cook.

ENVELOPE-
        Double Springs, Tenn
            June 8th

                    Col. Sebird Rhea
                        Mercer County M. O.
                            Princeton P. O.
        Seal.

P. S.
I hear since this was wrote that sister Elizabeth got a fall from a horse
Beast & is badly hurt in her hip so she cannot walk thiugh I have not seen
her.

Land Grant , July, 20, 1837, Recorded in Book H. Page 406 407.

Land Office for the Mountain District of Tennessee, Town of Sparta, White Co.

being entry No 777 in E. Takers Office Jackson County, Tenn. Dated Nov.14,

1831 by No 777, Jan, 9, 1830. Granted by the State of Tennessee unto Richard

F. Cock, tract containing 500 acres, Oct. 21, 1836, on Cans Creek, Beginning

at Joseph Ray's 100 acre South, to Samuel Maxwell, East of Bald Knob. The road

leading from Gainesboro to Sparta, North then of the place called Pall Ridge.

Test.   Newton Cannon, Gov. of Tennessee (Seal)

          At Nashville, Tenn, July, 20, 1837 and of the Independance

of the United States the 62nd   by Gov. N. Cannon

Luke Lee (Seal)

Secretary of State.

State of Tennessee No 14542, Know ye that in consideration of Military Service
performed by Daniel McDanile to the State of North Carolina Warrant 3086 dated
the 5th day of Dec, 1785 for 640 acres and entered on the 30th day of December,
1812 by 9791 there is granted by the State of Tennessee unto John Massa assignee
of the heirs of the said Daniel McDaniel, a certain tract or parcel of land containing 50 acres part of said warrant by survey bearing the date 20 day of September, 1814 lying in the first district of White County, on a branch of Glade
Creek waters of the Falling Waters and bounded as follows to wit:Beginning at
South West Corner of Henry Williams, running East then South by a small branch
Then North to the beginning with the hereditaments and appurtenances to have
and to hold the said tract or parcel of Landwith its appurtenances to the said
JohnMassa and his heirsforever. In witness whereof Joseph McMinn, Governor of
the State of Tennessee, have hereunto set his hand and caused the great seal of
the State to be affixed at Murfreesborough 1820, Independance of the United
States , the Forty Fourth.

                       By the Governor, Joseph McMinn
Daniel Graham, Sec.

Recorded in the Register's Office in Tennessee, Apr, 4, 1821

                       By Sterling H Lester, D. R.

State of Tennessee #14542
   John Massa, 50 acres, White County.

            Property of O. D. Massa, Cookeville, Tenn.

BOND: Know all men by thispresent that I am held andfirmly bound unto Sarah
Walles in the primal sum of Two hundred Dollars being for value received of
his I bound myself my heirs and assigns to her the said Sarah Walles his heirs
and assigns.
        The consideration of the above obligation is such that if the above bound
Jacob Young shall well and truly mark unto Sarah Walles, A good and Lawful right
unto surtain Tract or Parcel of land beginning at the beginning corner of a
seventy-acre tract ofland entered under warrant in the name of George Cullem
now enters in the name of James Carr running North and then to a dry branch then
down said branch through the lain between whar said Sarah Walles and Henry Carr
now lives, Till it stakes Rock Spring Creek then up said Creek to the beginning
then the above obligation to suposed to be Twenty three acres and one there be the
same more or less to be void otherwise toremain in full fore andvirtue, as
witness my hand and seal this day of July, 1834.
        The Right to be made so soon as a survey and Grant may be obtained.

                       Jacob Young (Seal)

                       James M. Kinly, (Seal)
For value received in full 2 asign over the within Bond toWade H Wallace,
this 30th of Apr, 1836
            Sarah Wallace (Her Mark)

H. L. McDaniel

            Sarah Walles Bond on Jacob Young & M Kinley.

Property Of O. D. Mason, Cookeville, Tenn.

The State of Tennessee No 7032.

To all to whom these presents shall come Greeting:
Know ye, that by virtue of part of Certificate No 1868, dated the 26th day of Augus
1814 essind by the Register of West Tennessee to Bennett Searcy and entered on the
27th day of August 1814 by No 13225, There is granted by the said State of Tennessee unto James Townsend, assignee of the said Bennett Searcy, A certain tract or parcel of land containing, One hundred and fifty acres by suevey bearing date the
12th day of January, 1815, lying in White County in the first District on Cane
Creek of the Falling Water, adjoining a survey of Isaac Taylor, Jun of four
hundred and two acres on his South boundry Beginning in his line at a post in
Cane Creek, Seventy poles of his beginning corner running South two hundred poles
to two black oaks thence West one hundred and Sixteen poles to a Chestnut and
hickory, thence North Striking the South East corner of Levi Sweats 100 acres
survey at eight poles containing North with Sweats line and crossing Cane Creek th
three times in all one hundred and eighteen poles to two post oaks, said Sweats
North East corner thence West with another of his lines ten poles to a postoak
thence North eighty two poles to a hickory post oak and black oak thence East striking the before mentioned corner of Isaac Tayler Junior, survey at eighty six
poles and crossing Cane Creek several times, in all one hundred and twenty six
poles to the Beginning, Including the farm and spring where Levi Sweats formerly lived, with the hereditaments and appurtenances, To have and to hold the said
tract or parcel of land with its appurtenances to the said James Townsend and his
heirs forever? In witness whereof Willie Blount, Govenor of the State of
Tennessee hath hereunto set his hand and caused the Great Seal of the State to
be affixed at Nashville on the twenty fourth day of May in the Year of Our Lord,
One Thousand and eight hundred and fifteen and of the Independance of the United
States the thirty ninth.

                              Willie Blount.

W. G. Blount,
        Secretary.

Shopping ninety years ago from an old day book of sales at the White Plains General
Store, the trading center for mant miles in every direction, we take the following
items entered in the year 1838-1840.

Joseph Bartlett

2¼ lbs coffee	. 50¢
2 Almanacks	.18

Robert Peek

One fine comb	.12½

Ann Quarles

One silk handkerchief	I.25
One nut meg	.06

William Marchbanks

2½ lbs lead	.3I
half dozen flints	.06

John Choat

Half pound powder	.25
2lbs lead	.25
3½ yds calico	.87½
half oz camphor	.I0
2 lbs sugar	.25

dudley Hudgens

8I lbs nails	I.00

Benjamin Gerdenhire

2 yds flannel	I.75
2 " calico	.67
¼ yd Bobinette	.18½
½ yd X-barred muslin	.37½
I tucking comb	.12½
I sett bridle leathers	I.00

Curtis terry

One pair cotton cards	.75
X yd domestic	.37½
One ribbon	.25
One fur hat	4.00

John Barnes after purchasing powderl lead, sugar and coffee adds one History of
United States One letter writer, four primers and one Charlotte Temple.
(Can any one shed any light on this last item?)

Copied from original account book of White Plains General Store, Book owned by
W. S. McClain, Cookeville, Tenn, Putnam County.

COPY OF WILL
OWNED BY MRS. MOLLIE McKINLEY, CHESTNUT MOUND, TENN.

State of Tennessee, Febuary Session, Jackson County of the County Court, 1834.

I William Gailbreath Clerk of the Court of Pleas and Quarter Session for said County do certify that Alfred Vannersen and Simon Carlisle executors of the last will and testiment of Robert McKinley deceased appeared in Court and were qualified as exicutors of said will and werepermitted to perform their duty as such without giving security according to said Wll in testimony where of I have set my hand and affixed the Seal of my office at office this 10, day of Febuary 1834

William Gailbreath, Clerk.

In the Name of God Amen I Robert McKinley of Jackson County andState of Tennessee being in sound mind and memory for whichI thank God and calling Mind the uncdrtainty of his mind and life and knowing that it is appointed once for all "men to die- and being desirous to dispose of such worldly substances asit hath pleased God to bless me with do hereby make my last will and testament in name and from following, that is to say,

1st I desire that after my death I shall be decently buried andall my Just debts be paid out of the prcoseds of my perishable property.

2nd-After hhe payment of my debts and furnel expenses I Give to my loving wife, Sally McKinley all the houses plantations Lands and stark of every discription whereon I now live and have and my negro woman Priss and all her children during her natural life and should she have more stock of any kind then she may needshe shall be at liberty to give it to either of my th three sons herein after named by value as low so as to make them equal in all such property I give away, and at her death my wish and will is that my negro woman Priss shall be set free and that she Priss may live with either of my children that she may make choice of-

3rd My wish and will is that at the death of my wife that my son Mathew Mck-Kinley shall have the tract of land and plantationwhereon I now live and no other part of my property from me.

4th-My wish and will is that my six negro children of Priss viz-Ned, Dick, Chind, Hanna, Lewis, & Milly be divided between my two sons James and Joseph in this manna Towit I desire that my son James shall have the two first choic and my son Josiah the two next and the balance equally divided between them

5th- My wish and will is that shallthere be any more I wish it or them be equally divided between my three sons and my wish is that should Priss have a any children she is freed or after my death it or they shall also be slaves and equally divided among my three sons before mentioned as I do not wish for someof her children to be free and the ballance slaves.

6th- My will and request of my beloved children is that these negroe here above mentioned shall be kept if possible in my family among my own children and never sold to strangers or any body else/

7th- My wish and will is that my house hold and kitchen furniture and farming utencels shall remin and belong to my wife during her natural life and at her death to be equally divided between my three sons by sale or otherwise as my Exicutors herein mentioned may think proper.

McKINLEY WILL (CON)

And lasly I do hereby constitute and appoint my true and faithful friends
Somin Carlisle and Alfred Vannerson Exicutors of this my last will and testament hereby working all other former will and testamentw nby me here to fore
made and my will and wish is that neither of these my exicutors shall be
bounded to give security and that they do perform the dutiesherein requirred
as soon as possableband without delay when my loving wife shall depart this 1
life In witness whereofI have set my hand and affixed my seal signed sealed
published and   Robert McKinley
declared to be the lastvwill and testament of the above nemed Robert MCKinley
In the presents of us who at his request and in his presence Have hereunto
subscribed our names as witness to the same this the fifth day of June one
thousand eight hundred and thirty.
Test-

     Simon Carlisle
     Alf Vannerson
     State of Tennessee, Jackson County, Febuary Session 1834
There was the last within will and testament of Robert McKinley Deceased in
Court for probate and Simon Carlisle and Alfred Vannerson subscribing witness
to saidlast will and testament beingsworn to testify teuching themaking
signing and publishing said will deposed and saidthat the Robert McKinley
signed said will in the presence and that at the time he signed it he was of
sound mind and disposing memory and en motion it is ordered that said will be
certified and recorded.

                                        William Gailbreath
                                        Clerk of Jackson County Court.

State of Tennessee, Jackson County, I William Gailbreath Clerk of the Court
of Pleasant Quarter Session for said County of Jackson do certify that the a
bove and foregoing is a true and pwefset Copy of last will and testamnt of
Robert McKinley by Deceased takenfrom the original on file inmyoffice and also
atrue and perfect copy of the entry of the probate ed said last will and te
testament taken from the record in my office, In Testimony Whereof I have
here unto set my hand and affixed the seal of my office in Gainesboro this
loth day of Febuary 1834

                                        William Gailbreath Clerk

     A copy of the last will and testament of R. M. McKinley dec.
     Original Records Book C. pages 313 & 314 in my office
                                        William Gailbreath Clk.)

RECORDS OF MRS. MOLLIE McKINLEY (CON)

State of Tennessee No 7273,
To all to whom these presents shall come, Greetings:

Know ye that for and in consideration of the sum of one cent per acre paid into the office of the Entry Taker of Jackson County and entered on the 245h day of Febuary 1826 pursuant to the provisions of an Act of General Assembly of said state passed on the twenty second day of November, one thousand and eight hundred and twenty three and the act supplemented thereto by No 904, there is this day granted by the State of Tennessee unto Mathew McKinley a certain tract or parcel of Land Containing One hundred sixty two and one half acres by survey bearing date the Second day of May, 1826 lying in said County on the ridge dividing the waters of Indian Creek of Cumberland River and Rock Spring Creek of the Caney Fork and bounded as follows to wit: Beginning at two sugar trees on the North side of rhe Walron Road su south with point of ridge on the waters of said Indian Creek Running thence East two hundred and twenty eight poles to three lynns growing out of the same rout in a hollow the waters of said Indian Creek Thence South crossing the Walton Road at 34 poles inall one hundred and fourteen poles to a sugar tree and four Lynns growing out of the same woods West side of a hill the waters of Rock Springs valley thence Waest two hundred and twentyeight poles to a stake Thence Northcrossing said Road in all one hundred and fourteen poles to the Beginning Encluding said McKinleys improvement known by the name of Mount Richardson With the hereditaments and appurtenances, To have and to hold the said Tract or parcel of Land with its appurtenances , to the said Mathew McKinley andhis heirs forever Inwitness whereof Samuel Houston Governor of the State of Tennessee hath hereunto setbhis hand and caused the Great Seal of the State to be affixed at Nashville on the twelfth day of November in the Year of Our Lord oneThousand eight hundred and twenty seven and of the independance of the United States the fifty second
By the Governor, James Houston

Danial Graham
Secretary.
Matthew McKinley is entitled to the within mentioned tract of Land
D. M. McGavock Register of
West Tennessee By
H. W. McGavock D. R.
Recorded in the Registers office of West Tennessee in Book No 9
Stith Harrison D. R.

No 7273 Matthew McKinley
162½ acres Jackson County

RECORDS OF MRS. MOLLIE McKINLEY (CON)

To Sarah Wallas and her heirs and assigns and All mans of persons what-
so ever In Testimony here unto have set my hand and seal this day and date
above written

                                                Jacob Young

Test=Simon Carlisle
      James McK,nley

                          LAND GRANT

     State of Tennessee No 7183
To all to whom these presents shall come Greetings:
Know ye that by virtue ofEntry No 1914 made in the office of the Entry
Taker of Jackson County and entered on the 13 day of August 1832 pursuant
to the provixions of an Act of General Assembly of S id State passed on the
ninth day of January 1830 there is Granted by the Said State of Tennessee
unto James McK,nley certain tract or parcel of Land containing one hundred
acres by survey bearing date rhe 27th day of March 1838 lying in said Coun-
ty ont the waters of Indian Creek of Cumberland River Bounded as follows:
Beginning at a poplar andchestnut Stump North East corner of a fifty acre
Entry made inthe name of said McKinley nara the Walton Road Running thence
West with said lineone hundred and sixty two poles to a stake thence North
one hundred and sixty poles to a Stake the East sixty poles to a large
Beech North West corner of a tract Granted Jordan Sullivan now belongs to
McClellan J,nes thence South with said tract crossing two branches in all
ninety six poles to a forked Lynn on the North side of a hill corner of sad
 tract thence East with said tract crossing two branches and a road from t
 the pond Spring passing beech corner of said tract at 94 poles in all one
hundred and two poles to a stake on the west side of a hill thence South
sixty four poles to the Beginning including the improvement purchased of
George Blair with the hereditaments and appurtenances to have and to hold
the said tract or parcel of land with its appurtenanc s tonthe said James Mc-
Kinley and his heirs forever, In witness of Newton Cannon Governor of the
State of Tennessee has hereunto set his hand and caused the great Seal of
the State to be affixed at Nashville on the 14th day of September 1839 and 64
year of our Independance

                                        By the Govnor
                                          James K. Palk
                                   Luke Lea
                                            Secretary

No 1387 James McKinley
          vs
B. F. Brinley etal
Exhibit No 1 to
  Disposition of
R. B. McKinley

 Filed May, 29, 1903, J. H. Watts Com.

Know all men by these presents That I Martin Brown of the County of Jackson and State of Tennessee am hheld?) and formly Bound unto James McKinley of the same County and State in the parcel sum of six hundred & dollars to which payment will and truly to be made and done I bine myself heirs executors and Administrators joinlty and severly firmly by these presents signed joinlty and severly firmly by these present signed with my name and sealed with my seal this 2nd day of Aprile in the Year of Our Lord 1830

The condition of the obligation is such that whenss the above Bounded Martin Brown hath this day bargained Sold and delivered unto said James McKinley the following tracts of Land To wit One hundred acres of land perchased by the said Brown of Hezakiah Brown and also one tractof fourteen acres purchased and one six acre tract perchased of said Hezakiah Brown also avtract of Onehundred which the said Martin Brown rendered at one cent per acre which is not yet surveyed and also One tract of fifty acres which was granted to the said Martin Brown by the State of Tennessee Under the act of General Assembly passed in 1823 commonly called the 12½ cts Law and also one tract offourteen acres which is of his own right to land that belonged to the estate of his father now Deceased Now Therefore Witnasseth That whereas the said Martin Brown holds a Bondon the said James McKinley fot three hindred dollars payable in the following manner towit One hundred dollars to be paid on or before the 20th day of Aprile 1831 One hundred dollars payable on or before the 20th day of Aprile 1832 and one hundred dollars payable on or before the 20th day of Aprile 1833 in consideration of the before mentioned an bargained premises now of the said Martin Brown shall well and truly make or cause to be made a General Warranted to the saidJames McKinley his heirs or assigns on or before the 20th day of Aprile 1831 Then this obligation to be a void else remain in full force and virtura

Martin Brown   (SEAL)

Witness Geo Elgin
Robert McKinley

Martin Brown
     To   Bond
  James McKinley

Know all men by these present s that James McKinley of the County of Jackson and State of Tennessee am held andfirmly bound unto Martin Brown of the Same County State in the Personal sum of Six hundred dollars to which payment well and truly to be made and done I bind my self my h heirs executors and Administrators Jpinlty and Severally firmly by them presents Sogned with my name and Sealed with my Seal this 20th day of April 1830

This condition of the all above obligation is such that when as the ab above bounded I James McKinley hath this day purchased of Martin Brown several tracts of land whereon the said Martin now lives which land s are discrebed in a bond from said Martin Brown bearing date the same date of this, Now therefore Witnesseth that wherever the said Martin Browm shalt mk make or cause to be made a General Warrantee deed or a good and sufficient title to the said James McKinley for the siad bargained p remises The said James McKinley bind himself to pay rhe said Martin Brown or his heirs three hundred dollars on the foll owing payments to wit One hundred dollars on or before the 20th day of Aprile in the year 1831 One hundred dollares on or before the 20th day of Aprile in the year of 1832 and also one hindred dollars on or before the 20th day of Aprile in the year 1833 Now if the said Brown sh shall make or cause to make a good and sufficient title for said lands and thes said McKinley Shall and trult make or cause to be made the three several payments of foresaid then this obligation to be void else remain in full forse and virtue

James McK┴nley   (SEAL)

Witness Geo Elgin
    James McK┴nley
        To Bone $00
M. BROWN

RECORDS OF MRS. MOLLIE McKINLEY (CON)

Jackson County State of Tennessee 27th Aprile 1831
   I do hereby certify that on the 17th day of March last I was on my way
from Summer County in this State to Warren County in North Carolina and
that I did on that day fall incompany with Mr. Johnson at a Mr. Bailleys
in Smith County in Smith County and that we then traveled to gether that
day and Staid that night at Mr. James McKinleys In Jackson County where
wecarrievd about night and found Mr. McKinley and Family from home—never—
theless we staid all night and was treated very well I slept in a little
room to the right hand as you enter the Big or publis room Mr. J hnson
shept in the public room by the fire in the morning after Breakfast we
paid our Bills to a little Boy Mr. McKonley's Son I suppose and was pursued our Journey on to gather as far as the forks of the Road where the
Walton Road leaves the Sparta Road about ten miles I suppose there we parted
and I had not heard from Mr. Johnson since till this evenong whenI called at
Mr. McKinleys on My return home and he Showed me an advertisement of Mr.
Johnson Stating that he had loss some money and his pocket Book at Mr Mc-
Kinleys on the night we staid there together now all this is entirely new to
me. I never heard Mr. Johnson say a word about such a thing while I was with
him—and as to any necessity of using any precaution while at Mr. McKinleys I
must confess I saw no need orCause of any apprehension . I further understand
that Mr. J hnson stated that he did not know my name orwho I was Now if this
be fact it is wrong as he both knew my name where I live and where I was going
and if any body wants to know I live in Summer County State of Tennessee Near
Hendersonville and my name
                                        Edward Turner
Is Witness Henry W. Kirby, Alf Vannerson

RECORDS OF MRS. MOLLIE McKINLEY (CON)

Design No 3 L. B.
  Pekin Putnam County Tennesse Oct. 9th 1873
I have this day bought of J. O. Pool and J. D. Clark marble Dealers No 72
West Jefferson St. Louisville, Ky. two set of "Italian Marble Grave Stone
Head Stone Marble 3½ feet high 18 inch wide 2 inch thick foot stone one
third as high and one thrid the width of Head Stone Bases for Head and
foot Stone Inscribed as follows:
  James McKinley Born June 5, 1894 —(1794?)
    Died Feb 5 1839

  Eliza McKinley Born Feb 1, 1800
    Died Mar, 22, 1871
to be delivered at Grandville on Cumberland River any time between the first
of Feb and the last of March next for which I agree to pay $70.00 Dollars on
Delivery
  (Now Putnam County Date Aug, 25, 1936)

  Know all men by these presents that I Samuel Wallace of Jackson County
State of Tennessee Pentioner ofthe United States do hereby causeth ? and
appoint James McKonley My yrue and Laeful attorney for me and in myName to
Bereve from the agent of the United States paying pensions in Nahsville
State of Tennessee my pention from the 4th day of Sectember 1834 to the
4th of March 1835 witness my hand and seal this 8th April1835
    Samuel Wallace X his mark (SEAL)
Lewis Fletcher Ely his Arleage

State of Tennessee , Jackson County, Be it known that on the 8th day of Aprile
1835 the Subscriber a Justice of the peace in fore said County personally appeared Samuel Wallace above named and acknowledgedThe foregoing power of
attorney to be his act and deed In Testimony whereofI have hereunto set my
hand this day and year Test above mentioned
    H. L. McDanial (SEAL)
    Justice of the peace.
State of Tennessee, Jackson County Be it known thathon the 8th day of Aprile
1835 before the subscribed a justice of the peace in and for said County per
sonally appeared James McK nley the attorney Name in the foregoing power of
attorney and made Oath that the same was not givenhim by reason of any sale
transfer and mortgage of pension therein anuther to be received by him
sworn and Subscribed the day and year last mentioned
 H. C. McDAnial,   James McK nley
  Justice of the Peace

RECORDS OF MRS. MOLLIE McKINLEY (CON)

State of Tennessee, Jackson County,
Be it knaoen that before me Henry L. McDanilea Justice of the peace in
and for the county aforesaid personally appeared Samuel Wallace and made
oath in due form of Law that he is the identical Wallace named in Brigonal
certificate in his posession of which I certify the following is a true
Copy.

War Department Revolutionary Claim

I certify that in Conformity with the Law of the United States of the 7th
Jan 1832 Samuel Wallace of the State if Tennessee who was a private in the
army of the Revolution is entitle to Eighty dollars per anam? during his
natural life comencing on the 4th March 1831 and payable SemiAnnually on
the 4th of March and 4th of September in every year.
Given at the War office of the United States this 19th day of March one
thousand Eight hundred and Thirty

Law Cass, Secretary of War

Examined and Countersign
   J. L. Edwards Commission of Pensions
th t he is entille to a pension of Eighty dollars per amm on account of
service rendered the Unoted States during the Revolutionary Warthat he re-
sides in Jackson County Tennessee and hasresided there fot the space of
Twenty six years past previous then he resided in Georgia Sworn and Subscribed before me this 8th day of Aprile 1835

H. L. McDanial
Samuel Wallace X His mark (SEAL)

State of Tennessee Jackson County, I Henry L. McDanial a magistrate in
the county above named do hereby certify that I have the most Satisfactory
Samuel Wallace who has this ady appear before me to take the oath of identi
ty is the identical person named in the pension Certificate which he has exhibited before me Number 20573 and bearing date at the war office the 19th
day of March 1834 and signed by Law Cass Secretary of War given under my
hand at Jackson County Tennessee on the 8th day of Aprile 1835

H. L. McDAnial (SEAL)
- Justice of the peace
State of Tennessee Jackson County, I J hn S. Turner Clerk of the County
of Jackson hereby certify that Henry L. McDanial is a magistrato as above
and that the foregoing Signature perporting to be his aregenuine in testimony whereof I hereunto set My hand andaffixed my Seal of Office this11th dayo
of April 1835

J. S. TurnerClerk of
Jackson County Court

Samuel Wallace
J. S. Turner Clk of Jackson County Court

RECORDS OF MRS. MOLLIE mMcKINLEY (CON)

State of Tennesse No 2913

To all to whom these presents shall come Greeting:

Know ye That for and in consideration of the sum of twelve and one half cents per acre paid into the office of the Entry Taker of Overton County and entered on the day of 27th of October 1824 pursuant to the provisions of an Act of General Assembly of said State passed on the twenty second of November one thousand eight hundred and twenty three by No 391 There is Granted by the said State of Tennessee unto Henry McKinney a certain tract or parcel of Land containing Fifty Acres by survey bearing date the 23rd day of July 1825 lying in said county on the waters of Bear Creek and bounded as follows to wit: Beginning at a stake a post oak and small hickory Running South Eighty poles to a small black oak and Black Jack thence East one hundred poles crossing the rock Island read to a small Stake a small hickory and post oak Thence North Eighty poles crossing said road to two small Hickorys Thence West one hundred poles to the Beginning

With the hereditaments and appertenanses To have and to hold the said tract or parcel of Land with its appertenances to the said Henry McKinney and his heirs forever. In witness whereof William Sarroll Govnor of the State of Tennessee hath hereunto set his hand and caused the Great Seal ot the State to be affixed at Murfreesborough on the 21st day of November in the Year of Our Lord one thousand eight hundred and twenty five and of the Independance of the United States the fiftieth

By the Govnor—Wm Carroll

Daniel Graham Secretary

Recorded in the Reg Office of West Tennessee 21st March 1826 C

H. W. McGavock D. R.

No 2913 Henry McKinney 50 acres Overton County

Henry McKinney is entitle to the within mentioned tract

D. McGavock Registered of West Tennessee

State of Tennessee No 2918

To all to whom these presents shall come Greeting:

Know ye, That for and in consideration of the sum of Twelve and one cent per acre paid into the office of the Entry Taker of Overton County and entered on the 15 th day of Aprile 1824, pursuant ot the provisions ef an Act of General Assembly of said State , passes on the twenty second day of November one thousand eight hundred and twenty three by No 36 there is granted by the said State of Tennessee unto Nathan Bartlett a certain tract or parcel of Land containing sixty six acres of survey bearing date the 10th day of June 1825 lying in said County on the waters of Bear Creek whereon Henry McKinney now lives and bounded as follows to wit: Beginning at a two postoaks Running South seventy four poles to two small blavek oaks and Hickory pointers Thence East one hundred and forty three poles to a small black oak at the foot of a mountain Thence North seventy four poles to a small hickory and post oak thence west one hundred and forty three poles to the Beginning with the hereditaments and appurtenences To have and to hold the said tract or parcel of Landwith its appertenances to the said Nathan Bartlett In witness whereof William CarrollGovnor of the State of Tennessee heth hereunto set his hand and caused the Great Seal of the United States to be affixed at Murfreesborough on the 21st day of November in the Year of Our Lord one thousand eight hundred and twenty five and of the Independance of

RECORDS OF MRS. MOLLIE McKINLEY (CON)

the United States the fiftieth

             Bybthe Govnor William Carroll

             Daniel Graham, Secretary

Nathan Bartlett is entitled to the within mentioned tract of land

              D. W. McGavock Register of West Tennessee

No 2918 Nathan Bartlett 66 acres Ovetton County

Recorded in the Registers office of West Tennessee 22nd March 182 C

                D. W. McGavock D. R

RECORDS OF MRS. MOLLIE McKINLEY (CON)

State of Tennessee No 6829

To all to whom these presents shall come Greetings: Know ye that for and in consideration of the sum of one Cent per acre paid into this office of the Entry Taker of Overton County and entered on the 9th day of January, 1826 pursuant to the provisions of an Act of the General Assembly of said State and passed on this 3 day of December 1825 by No 544 made in said office there is granted by the said Sate of Tennessee unto Henry McKinley a certain Tract or parcel of land containing Two hundred acres by survey bearing date the 16th day of May 1838 Lying in said Countynof on the head waters of Bear Creek Beginning at a small hickory the Barrens on the North boundry line of 66 acres Tract whereon said McKinnley now lives Running North Seventy poles to a small hickory and post ack ThenceEast 60 poles to two small Hickorys at the foot of a mountain thence South with the same thirtyeight poles to a white oak and chestnut thence East with the same tenements six poles to a black walnut and hickory South with the same 12 poles to a small hickory and black oak pointers Thence East One hundred and Eighty poles to a Spanish Oak and two chestnuts pointers Thence South one hundred and thirty and two thirds poles to a Stake thence East west two hundred and twenty poles to a stake thence North one hundred and nine poles binding on the East boundry line of said 66 acres Tract to a Small hickory and post oak and pointers the North East corner of the same West with North boundry of the same forty poles to the Beginning with the hereditaments and appurtenences to have and to hold the aid Tract or parcel of land with its appurtenences to the said Henry McKinley and his heirs forever.

In witness whereof Newton Cannon Govnor of the State of Tennessee has hereunto set his hand and caused the Great Seal of the State to be affixed at Nashville on the 2nd day of May 1839 and 63 Year of our Independance

By the Govnor, N. Cannon

Luke Lea

Secretary

Reg. in the office Book M. Page 97

R. Nelson Reg. Mountain District

Henry McKinley is entitled to the within described Land

R. Nelson, Reg.

No 6827

Henry McKinley 200 acres

The State of Tennessee No 7591
To all to whom these presents shall come Greetings:
Know ye that by virtue of part of Certificaye No 1591 dated the
9th day of September 1813 issued by the Register of West Tennessee to
Robert Searly and entered on the 17th day of September 1813 by No 11438
There os granted by the said State of Tennesse Unto Eake Brown assignee
of the said Robert Searly a certain tract or parcel of Land canteining
four teen acres by survey bearingdate the 30th day of Aprile 1814 Lying
in Jackson County in the first District on a branch of Indian Creek of
Cumberland River and bounded as follows to wit Beginning at a branch Standig
three poles West of the North East corner of said Brown survey of fourteen
acres on said branch running North forty eight poles to a Spanish oak and
Small white oak thence West forty seven poles passing the South East corner of said Browns survey of six acres at fifteen poles and with said line to
a stake in a filed thence South forty eight poles to a sugar tree thence
East forty seven poles te a forty eight poles to a sugar tree thence East
firty seven poles to the Beginning. With the heredotaments and appurtenanc
to have and to hold the said tract or parcel of land with its appurtenencest
to the said Eake Brown andhis heirs forever in witness whereof
Willie Blount Govner of the State of Tennessee hath hhtsunto set his hand
nand caused the grear seal of the State to be affixed at Nashville on the
Seventeenth day of Aug in the Year fo Our Lord one thousand Eight hundfed
and fifteen and of the Independance of the United States the Fortieth
                                        Willie Blount
                                        By the Govnor

W. T. Blount
        Secretary
Received in the Registers office of West Tennessee Sept 11th 1815
                                        D. M. McGavock Reg

No 7591 Eale Brown
14 acres
Jackson County.

        State of Tennessee No 7187
To all to whom these shall come Greetings:
Know ye that by virtue o f Entry No 2499 Made in the office of the Entry
Taker of Jackson County and entered on the 22nd day ofMarch 1837 pursuant to
the provisions of an act of the General Assembly of said state passes on th
the ninth day of January 1830 there is warrented by the said state of Tenn
essee unto James McKinley a certain tract er parcel of land containing
Twenty five acres by survey beaing date the 30 day of March 1838 lying in
said County on the South sidedof Cumberland River on the waters of Indian
Creek Beginning at a Bumbhand Elm on the South side of Indian Creek corner of a tract G anted to Isaac Walton Running thence West with said tract
twenty poles to a Stake thence East 20 poles to a Stake in the West boundryl
line of Matthew Cowins tract thence North with said line two hundred poles
to the Beginnijg including the improvement bought of Henry B. Clark bt said
McKinley
No 7181 James McKinley 25 acres Jackson County
Recorded in my office Book L. Page 152
                                        R. Nelson, Register of the Mountain District

RECORDS OF MRS. MOLLIE McKINLEY (CON)

The State of Tennessee No 7592-
To all to whom these presents Shall come Greetings:
Know ye that by virtue of part of cretificates No 472 dated the first day
of January 1811 obtained from the commisiioner of West Tennessee by Arin
Robertson Elizabeth Robertson Christopher Robertson and Mary Robertson and
entered on the 11th day of January 1812 by No 7432 There is granted by the
said state of Tennessee unto Eape Brown assignee of said Ann Robertson Jas
Robertson Elizabeth Robertson Christopher Robertson Elijah Robertson and
Mary Robertson a certain tract or parcel of land containing fourteen acresb
by survey baring date the 30th day of Aprile 1814 lying in Jackson County
in the first district on a branch of Indian Creek of Cumberland rover and
boundes as follows to wit-Beginning at a branch marked E. B. about ten poles
East of said branch and thirty poles above an improvement made by Meshack
Hanbery runs thence West forty poles crossing said branch to a sugar tree
thence South fifty six poles to a sugar tree thence East forty poles to a
lynn and two sugar trees Saplings on the bank of a branch thence North fifty six poles to the Beginning Including the improvements where said Brown
now lives. With the hereditaments and appurtenances to have and to hold the
said tract or parcel of land with its appurtenances to the said Eake
Brown and his heirs forever in witness where of Willis Bleunt Govner of the
State of Tennessee hath sey his hand and caused the great Seal of the State
to be affixed at Nashville on the Seventeenth day of August in the Year of
Our Lord one thousand Eight hundred and fifteen and of the Independence of
the United States the fortieth
      By the Govnor,
        Willie Blount

William Blunte
  Secretary
No 7592 Eake Brown 14 acres Sept 11, 1815 Jackson County
Recorded in the Register's office of West Tennessee B.
Eake Brown is entitled to the within mentioned tract of land
      D.-M. McGavock Register,
      West Tennessee.

RECORDS OWNED BY MRS. MOLLIE MCKINLEY, CHESTNUT, MOUND, TENN.

State of Tennessee No 702,
To all to whom these presents shall greetings:
Know ye, that for and in consideration of the sum of twelve and one halfa
cents per acre Paid into the office of the Entry Taker of Jackson County d
and entered on the 5 day of the July 1823pursuant to the provisions of an
Act of the General Assembly of said state,passed on the 22nd day of Novem
ber 1823 by No 305,
There is granted by the State ofTennessee unto Andrew Ferrell a certain
tract or parcel of Land containing fifty acres by survey bearing date the
18th of November, 1824 laying in said county on a branch of Indian Creek on
South side of Cumberland river and bounded as follows: Beginning at an elm
in the West bound thirty poles North of the beginning corner of said Ferrell 98 acre tract Running thence Seen a one hundred and twenty five poles to
stake in Robert McKinley's field twenty five poles to a stake in Robert Mc-
Kinley's field thence West Sixty four poles to a tract thence North one hund
dred and twenty five poles to an elm thence East sixtyfour poles to the
beginning.
With the hereditaments and appurtenances To have and to hold the said
Tract or parcel of Landwith its appurtenances, to the said Andrew Ferrell
and his heirs forever In Witness whereof William Carroll, Govnor of the stat
of Tennessee, hath hereunto set his hand and caused the Grent Seal to be affix
ed at Murfreesboro on the 7th day of Janutary, In the Year of Our Lord one t
thousand eight hundred and twenty five and of the Independance of the United
States the forty-ninth.

By the Govnor
Daniel Graham
Secretary
Wm. Carroll

Recorded in the Registers office of West Tennessee May, 28, 1825.
W. M. McGavock
D. R^{E}g.

No 702

Andrew Ferrell
50 acre
Jackson County.

RECORDS OF MRS. MOLLIE McKINLEY (CON)

State of Tennessee No 727
To all to whom these presents shall come, greetings:
          Know yea, That for and in consideration of the sum of twelve and
one cents per acre paid into the office of the Entry Taker of Jackson
County and entered on the 25th day of June 1824 pursuant to the provision
of an Act of General Assembly of said State passed on the 22 day of Nov.
1823 by No 130, There is granted unto Martin Brown a ceratin tract or parcel of Land containong fifty acres by survey date the 1st day of July 1824
lying in Said county on the waters of Indian Creek on the South Side of
Cumberland River and bounded as follows to wit Beginning at a small beach
on the West side of a hill thence West fifty poles to a stake in the
east boundry line of Eake rown 14 acre tract thence South with line thirty
six poles to his South East corner thence West with his lune passing his
corner in all sixty thence est wth his line passing his corner in all
sixty poles to a Stake rhence South fifty four poles three and thence
four poles to a stake thence east one hundred and twelve poles to a stake
thence North ninty & three fourth of a pole to the Beginning,
With the hereditamenets and appurtenances To haveand to hold the said
Tract or parcel of Land with ist appurtenences to the said Martin Brown an
his heirs forever, In witness William Carroll Govnor of the State of Tennessee hath hereunto set his hand andcaused the GreatSeal of the State to
be affixed at Murfreesborough on the 11 day of January in the Year of Bur
Lord one thousand and eight hundred and twenty five and of the Independane
of the United States for the forty ninthBy the Gonvor
                              Daneil Graham
                                   Secretary
               Wm. Carroll

No 727
Martin Brown 50 acres Jackson County
Recorded in the Registers office of West Tennessee May 30th 1825
               M. Gavock, D. Regt

          Know all men by these pasnts(?) are held & privy reviel unto Jane
Wallam fenal sum of six hundred & Twenty four dollars the consider od this
obligation is such that the said shall make or cause to be made by way of
general Transaction deed on the 20 day of January 1844 to Jane Jane
Wallam a certain tract or parcel land containing seventy four acres lying
in the State of Tennessee and County of Putnam on the waters of Indian
Creek of Cumberland River and bounded as follows Beginning at a lynn on
the road the North East Corner of Lot No 5 surveying thence North sixty thee
poles to a beech standing near the Road thence North seventy four and a
half degrees thence one hundred and Thirty four poles to a sugar tree on the
top of the rodge thence South thirty degrees thence runningthe ridge sixty
eught poles to a small Beech a hickory & maple pointers thence South with the
ridge twenty four poles to a stake in the N. Boundry line of Sam Young fifty
trail thence East with Sam Young fifty acre tract thence East with said
Youngs line thirty poles to a sugar tree the N. corner of Lot No 5 thence East
fifty poles to a sugar tree in the North boundry line of Lot No 5 thence

RECORDS OF MRS. MOLLIE McKINLEY (CON)

South survey six degrees Ea st Eighty eight poles to the Beginning
There this obligation to the round or thence to the main in full form
in Law & equally in witness where here set my seal affixed my seal this
26 day of December 1843 in pen of therein Sarah McKinley

        Witness Robert G. Hufey   (SEAL)

Test—John Kovirs   Elijah McKinley (X his mark)
    Fichecher
S. M. McK^lnley P. G. & Hayhs
    To Bond J. Wallam

State of Tennessee No 740
To all to whom these presents shall come Greetings:
      Know yea that for and in consideration of the sum of one cent per
acre paid in the office of the Entry Taker of Jackson County and enter
thereon the 13th day of January 1826 pursuant to the provisions of an Act
of the General Assembly of sid State passed on the 3rd day of December
One thiysand ight hindred and twenty five by No 75G there is Granted by
the said State of Tennessee unto Hezakiah Brown a certain tract or parcel
of land lying containing two hundred acres by survey bearing date th
14th day of Dec. 1826 Lyingnin said County ont ehwaters of the Indian
Creek of Cumberland River and Bounded as follows Beginning ata Beech
Maple and sugar tree on the South side of a hill near the head fo a Small
branch that runs through his field and not far abpve a Spring running tha e
North One hundred and twenty six and one half poles to a Beech and dogwood
in the South boundry line of Gifien Browns fifty acre tract Thence East
with his line crossing a branch at fifty two poles ian all fifty two pole
in all two bundred and fifty two poles to a lage chestnut and two m ples
on the top of a high ridge Thense South one hundred and twenty six and one
half poles to a Dogwood and two pepulars sapling on the point of a ridge
not far above Jordan Sullivans fence thence West twohundred and fifty three
poles to the Beginning. With the hereditaments and appurtenances To have
and to hold the said Tract or parcel of land with appurtenances to the said
Hezakiah Brwon and his heirs forever In iwtness whereof Sam Houston Govnor
of the State of Tennessee hath hereunto set his hand and caused the great
S al of the State to be affixed at Nashville on the 14th day of August in
teh Year of Our Lord One thousand Eight hundred and twenty eight and of
the Independance of the United States th e Fifty third
        By the Govnor James Houston

Daniel Graham
    Secretary
Hezakiah Brown is entitle to the within described Land R. Nelson Register
of the Miauntain District Recorded in my office In Book 13 page 172
        R. Nelson
        Reg of the Mountain District

No 740 Hezakiah Brown 200 acres Jackson County
Isd 14 Aug 1828

McKinley Records (Con)

Know all men by these presents thatI Andrew Ferrell, of Jckson County
and state of Tennessee of some title and firmly bounded in the sum of
Three hundred dollars unto Robert Moore or heirs and each other and adminis
trators or assigns for each payment will and truly be made and Bind myself
my exicutors administrators jointly and severly formerly by this presents
sealed with my seal and dated the 20th of Feb. 1836 the conditions of
above obligation is such that if the above bounded Amdrew Ferrell orhis airs
Exicutors administrators make over all his rite and title unto sementy five
acres of land lying in the County of Jackson and on the waters of Indian
Creek and beginning on a large chestnut and two mapleson the top of a ridge
it being the North East corner of said tract of Land running thence west
to a stake on the top of a ridge North East corner of a tract of Land sold
byHezekiah Brown to Marlin Brown thence South corner with said Marlin Brown
line meandering to said ridge to a stake on the South Boundryline thence East
on said line seventy poles to a stake James McKinley South East corner on a
twenty five acre tract thence North with said McKinley line sixtu four poles
to a stake thence east with McKonley line sixty four poles to a stake in the
last Boundry line thence with said line to the Beginning unto RoberthMoore
his airs administrators thence the above obligation to be voyd other virtue
in law in witness untill I have set my hand and seal this day and date above
written

                                        Andrew Ferrell (SEAL)
  bind sealed and Delivered in presents of Jefferson Ferrell
Asign the with Bond to James McKinley Jaceb Young for value received of them
as witness my hand and seal this the 13th of March 1837
                                        Robert Moore (SEAL)

  and Ferrell to Bond to Robert Moore

RECORDS OF MRS. MOLLIE McKINLEY (CON)

This Indenture made this 23rd day of July in the year of Our Lord One thousand and Eight hundred and thirty Between Hezekiah Brown of the County of Jackson and State of Tennessee of the one part and William Collins of the same county andState of the other part witness with That said Hezakiah Brown aforesaid and consideration of the sum of Seven dollars and fifty cent in handpaid the receipt whereof is hereby acknowledged hath G,ven Granted bargain Sell amd deliver unto the Said William Collins a certain tract plase or parcel of Land Situated lying and being in the County of Jackson of said on the waters of Indian Creek it being a part of the State of Tennessee to the Hezakiah Brown by Bearingdate the 14th day of August in the year 1828 and nembered 740 and Beginning on a Large Chestnut and two Maples on the top of a Ridge it being the North east corner of said tract of Land Running tnence Westvtoa stake on the top of a ridge the North east corner of a tract of Land sold by said Hezakiah Brown toMartin Brown thence to Southern Cotrner with said Martin Browns line meadows the Said Ridge to a stake in the South Boundry line thenceeast on south line to sixty poles to a take James McKinley South east corner of a twenty five acre tract purchased of the said Hezakiah Brown thence North with said McKinley line sixty four poles to a stake his north esat corner thence east with said McKinley Boundry line sixty four poles to a stake in the east boundry line of the original survey thence North with said line to Beginning containing by Estimayion Seventy five acres be the same now or less togetherwith the Hereditaments and appurtenances to him the sia d William Collins his heirs and assigns forever and the said Hezakiah Brown for himself & his heirs doth hereby covenent and agree to ans with the said William Collins that he will forvevr warrant and defend the title of the above bargained premises to him he said William Collins his heirs and assigns forever from the lawful claim of any person or persons whatsoever InTestimony whereof the said Hezakiah Brown hath hereunto set his hand Seal the day and date first hand Seal the date first above written

James McK nley Hezakiah Brown

(SEAL)

Gro Elgin

Hezakiah Brown
To Deed 75 acres
William Collins

RECORDS OWNED BY MRS. MOLLIE MCKINLEY, CHESTNUT MOUND, TENN

This Indenture made this 21st day of July in the Year of Our Lord one
thousand Eight dundred and thirty Between Hezekiah Brown of the County of
Jackson and State of Tennessee of the one part and James McKinley of the
State and county aforesaid of the other partwitnesseth That the saidHezekih
Brown for and in considerationof the sum of One hundred dollars to him an
Land paid by the said McKinley the receipt whereof is hereby acknowledged
hath given granted bargained and sold and delivered and by these presents
doth give Grant bargained sold and delivered to the said James McKinley
his heirs and assigns a certain price parcel or tract of land situated
lying and being in the County of Jackson of said on the waters of IndianC
Creek Beginning on a Dogwood and Two poplar Sapling Running thense North
Sixty four poles to a stake thence West sixty three poles to a steak
thence South sixty four poles to a steak thence East to the Beginning
continuing twenty five acres it being the South East corner of the trad
of Land of Two hundred acres granted by the State of Tennessee tonthe
said Hezekiah Brown by protest Bearing datedate the First day of August,
1828 and Numbered 740 which said tract includes a part of the plantation
that George Blair formerly owned Together with the Hereditaments and ap-
purtenancesthereunto belonging to him the said James McKinley and hisheirs
and assigns forever and said Hezekiah Brown for himself and his heirs
doth hereby covenant and agree toand with said James McKinley that he wil
forever warrant and defend the title of th above premises from the lawfulc
claim or claims of all persons what so ever lawfully claiming the same to
be the said James McKinley his heirs and assigns forever In Testimony where
of the said Hezekiah Brown Hath hw re unto set his hand and Seal the day a
and date tfirst above written
Witnesses present
The words " a part of" Intered before assigned

                                    Hezekiah Brown (SEAL)

                                    William Collins X his mark
                                    Geo. Elgin

Hezekiah Brown
   Deed 25 acres
James McKinley

This endenture made and entered into this The twentieth day of November one thousand Eight hundre and thirty fiveBetween JacobYoung of the
one part and Sarha Wallas all of the County of Jackson and State of Tenne-
see Witnesses that the said Jacob Younghath bargained and sold and by these
presents do the bargain and sell To said Sarah Wallas a surtain Tract or
parcel of land lying and being in Jackson County on th South bank of Rock
Spring Beginning at the corner of seventy acre Tract Entered in name of
George Cullom Beginning on an ash and oak thence West To the first dry
branch and thence down the meadewsbof said ranch a long a Lain deviding betw
tween Sarah Wallas and Henry Carr thense up said Rock Springs To the Begin-
ningsupposed to be Twenty three acres and one third be the same more or less
which trail of land I do warrent and defend from me my Heirs and assigns,

RECORDS OF MRS. MOLLIE MCKINLEY (CON)

State of Tennessee, No 1498
To all to whom these Presents shall Come, Greetings :
 Know ye, that for and in consideration of the sum of one cent pwer acre
paid into the office of the Entry Taker of Jackson County and entered on
the 13th day of January 1826 pursuant to the provisions of anAct of the Gen
eral Assembly of said Tstate passed on the day fo December one thousand
and eight hundred and twenty five No 758 there is granted by the State of
Tennessee unto Thomas Gillehan a certain tract or parcel of land containing
Fufty acres by survey bearing date the Fourteenth day of December 1826 lying in said County on Young's fork of Indian Creek South side of Cumberland
River and boundes as follows Beginning at a sugar tree in the South boundryl
line of his one hundred acre tract on the point of a ridge not far from his
house and about sixty four poles East of his South West corner Running thence
South soxty poles to an elm in the North boundry line of Gideon Brown 50 acre
Tract Thence East with his line twelve poles to his North east corner a beech
Thence South with his line twenty two poles to a hickery Thence east seventy
 two ploes to a hickory a sugar tree in the West boundry line of Robert Mc-
Kinley 50 acre T act thence West passing his North west corner at thirty pole
in all one hundred and five and one half poles to two sugar trees Thence West
 fiftybeight poles to a sugar tree in the East boundry line of said William
Tract of one hundred acre Thence South with his line twenty three and one
half poles to a suger tree his corner Thence West with his line twenty six
poles to the beginning, With the Hereditaments and appurtenances To have and o
hold the said tract or parcel of land with its appurtenances tot ehs aid
Tomas Gillehan and his heirs forever, In witness where of WilliamnCarroll
Governor of the State of Tennessee has hereunto set his hand and caused the
great seal of theState to be affixed At Nashville on the 14th day of November
 intthe Year of Our Lord one thousand eight hundred and twenty nine and of
the Independance of the United States the fifty fourth
       By GovernorWm. Carroll
       Daniel Graham Secretary

No 1498
Thomas Gillehan Fify acres Jackson County
Recorded in my office Book C page 331
    R. N. NELSON Register of the Mountain District

PROPERTY OF MRS. DAVE HIGH, COOKEVILLE, TENN.
DEED.

Tis indenture made this 10th day of Dec., the Year of our Lord One thousand
eight hundred and twenty six, Between James Ray of the County of Jackson and
the State of Tennessee of the one part and John Ditty of the County of White,
and State foresaid of the other part witnesseth , that the said James Ray,
hath for the consideration of the sum of one hundred and sevwnty dollars to
him in hand paid the receipt whereof is hereby acknoeledged and there witg sat
isfied and content, hatn this day bargained and conveyed unto the said John
Ditty his heirs and assigns forever a certain tract or parcel of land con
taining by estimation one hundred acres, the same more or less, lying and
being on the County of Jackson and State afores and on the waters of Cane
Creek, it being the place whereon the said Ray now lives, butted and bounded
as follows, viz; Beginning at a Spanish oak it being the North west corner of
sd. tract runnung then South, one hundred and eighty eight poles ro a Steak h
thence West Eighty six poles to the beginning, To have and to hold the above
described land and bargained premices with all the propertyemeluments and appw
urtenances thereunto belonging or in any wise appertaining to the land I
hereby bind myself and my heirs and executors to warrent and forever defend
the right of said land from all and every person or persons claiming or to
claim the sam or any part thereof. In witness I have here unto set my hand
and affirmed my seal this day and date above written in presence of us,

James Ray (X his mark)

Test
W? M. Peak, Wm. I. Ray   A C td, 19th Nov, 1839

State of Tennessee, Registered Office, Feb, 10, 1840, Jackson County,
I, Saml. E. Hare, Reg. of said County do hereby certify that the within and
foregoing deed of conveyance from James Ray to John Ditty to Gather with the d
clerk, certificates is all duly Reg. in my Office Book E & R 435 & 426.

Sam E. Hare, Reg. Jackson Co.
State of Tennessee, Jackson County , Personally appeared before me John T.
Turner, clerk of the county court of Jackson , I am Ray the bargner or with
whom I am personally acquainted and who acknowledges this the granted within
and for the purpose herein contained, witness my hand at office, 19th Nov, 1839

J. S. Turner Clk.

DEED.

This Indenture made this 15th day of Dec, One Thousand Eight Hundred and
twenty six, Between George Carson, of the city of Baltimore and State of
Maryland by his Attorneys in fact Nehemiah Carsons of the County of Butler
and State of Kentucky of the part, and James and Matthew McKinley of the coun
ty of Jackson and State of Tennessee of the other part, witnessed that the
said George Carson by his Attorney Nehemiah Carson for and in consideration
of the sum of Five hundred dollars in hand paid the receipt whereof is here
by acknowledged hath granted, Bargained and sold unto the said James & Mat
thew McKinley a certain tract or parcel of Land containing Fifty acres lying
and being in the said county of Jackson on the Walton Road including the plan
tation and possession known by the name of Roulstons Stand or Mount Richardson
agreeable to the Entry made fot the same bounded as follows, viz; Beginning t
a Sugartree running Eighty nine poles to a Beech thence S. eighty nine poles
to a Line thence W. eighty nine poles to a stake thence N. eighty nine poles

DEED (CON)

to the Beginning. Also one other tract or parcel of Land int eh County and
State aforesaid containing Twenty acres Biunded as followsto wit: Beginning at
a sugar tree on the Ridge near where the path leading from Shadwick Bridges
intersects theWalton Road running thence N. forty polms to an elm & sugar twie
thence W. eight poles to a Dogwood & Ash, thence S. forty poles to a Beech &
Dogwood thence E. eighty poles to the Beginning. To have and to hold that
abound described Tracts and Bargained premices unto the said James & Mwtthews
McKinley three heirs and assigns forever and he the said George Carson by his
Attorney in fact Nehemiah Carson, does for himself his heirs and assigns forever warrent and defend the right and title claim and interest of the said prim
mices to the only proper use and behalf of the said James & Matthews McKinley
their heirs and assigns forever In witness whereof the said George Carson by h
his Attorney in fact Nehemiah Carson hath hereunto set his hand affixed his
seal the day and date above written .

                                        Nathen Carson, Attr in fact
                                        for ex Carson (Seal)

    Signed, sealed and Ack in presence of
        Rich M Cornwell
        James Carson
        John Pace

At a County Court Began and held at the Court house in the Morgantownon Monday
12, day of Feb. 1827 the forgoing Indenture of Bargain estate from Nehemiah
Carson all in part for George Carsen to James & Matthews McKinley was inopen
court proven to eb the act of sd. Carson, Testimony whereof I have here unto
set my hand at office the seal of said County Court, Feb. 12, 1827.and in the
35year, commondcults.

                            R. O. E. Morrison, Clerk,
                            State of Kentucky, Butler County.
        McKinley To Amonet, Fixed near 1888.

Property - Mrs. Davey Nichols, Ensor, Tenn
and Mrs. Dave High, Cookeville, Tenn

The State of Tennessee,
    To all to whom these presents shall come, Greeting.
    Know ye that in consideration of Entry No. 1652, made in the office of
the Entry Taken of Jackson County and Entered on the 16th day of Feb, 1830
pursuant to the provisions of an act of the General Assembly of said State passed
on the (th day of January , 1830. There is granted by the said State of Tennessee
unto William Brown a certain tract or parcel of land containing fifty acres by
survey bearing date the 27th day of April 1833 lying in Jackson County on the
waters of Martins Creek, Beginning at a Beech North of Peter Crooms Improvement
    running North sixty four poles to two Beeches and a White Oak, thence East one
hundred and twenty five poles to a Chestnut and Black gum, Thence South sixty
four poles to a Hickory and a Chestnut Oak on a ridge , Thence West one hundred d
and twenty five poles to the Beginning, including John Morgan Sugar Camp with
the hereditaments and appurtenances, To have and to hold the said tract or
parcel of landwith the hereditaments and appurtenances, To have and to hold
the said tract or parcel of landwith its appurtenances to the said William Brown
and his heirs forever
    In witness whereof Neil S. Brown, Govner of the said State of Tennessee
hath hereunto set his hand and caused the great Seal of the State to be affixed
at Nashville on the 25th day of Aug in the year of Our Lord One thousand and
eight hundred and forty nine and of the Independance of the United States the
Seventy Fourth Year,
                                    W. B. A. Ramsey, Secretary.

I, M. F. O'Conner Register of the Mountain District do hereby certify that the abv
above is a true and perfect transcript of grant No. 10176 for 50 acres Granted to
William Brown as appears on record in my office in the Book W. Page 694.
        Given under my hand at office the 23rd day of April A. D. 1870
                            M. F. O'Conner Regr Of the Mountain Dis.

Copy of Grant No. 10176
    William Brown
        50 acres
Jackson County.

Property Mrs. Dave Nichols, Ensor, Tenn also
Mrs. Dave High, Cookeville, Tenn.

82

We, William Jared and Matthew Jared have this day bargained and soldand do hereby
transfer and convey toMalinda Jared and his heirs foeever for the consideration o
of ten dollars to us paid a tract of land in the State of Tennessee , Jackson Couny
and laying on the waters of Indian Creek of Caney Fork containing by estimation
thirty acres be the same more or less and bounded as follows, beginning where the
East boundry line of a forty five acre tract granted to William Jared Dec, II
crossed the North fork of said Indian Creek running thence Eastward with the South
bank of said Creek to the mouth of a branch running into the South side of said
Creek thence South Easterdly with said branch to where the first left hand fork ofs
said branch thence Eastwardly to the east boundry line of a 75 acre tract granted
to William J red thence North to the North East cormer of said 75 acre tract
thence West to the North Bank of said Creek thence Westwardly with the North fork d
of said Creek to the beginning to have and hold the same to the said Malinda
Jared her heirs and assigns forever.

We do covenant and bind ourselves and heirs I representatives to warrent and
defend the title of the said land to Malinda Jared her heirs and assigns forever
against every claim to be made by ourselvesor any persons claiming through or
under us, but no farther this IIth day of Nov. 1839-Signed and delivered in the
presence of

                              William Jared(Seal)
                              Mat. R. Jared (Seal)

William R. Vance

Lawrence Byrne Jared, Nov, IIth, 1839.

  State of Tennessee, Jackson County
      Personally appeared before me John S. Tiuner, Clerk of the County Court of
County of Jackson, Tennessee, Byrne a subscribing witness tot he within deed
who being first sworn depose and say he is acquainted with William Jared and
Martha R. Jared the bargainors and that he saw them sign and heard them acknowl-
edge the execution of the same to be their act and deed for the purpose herein cont
tained and upon the day it bears date witness my hand at office this 19th dany of
Nov. 1839,
                              J. S. Turner, Clerk.
State of Tennessee, Jackson County,
      Personally appeared before me Alex Montgomery Clerk of the County Court of
Jackson County, William R. Vance a subscribing witness to the within deed named
and who being first sworn depose and say that he is acquainted with William Jared a
and Mat. R. Jared the bargainors and that they acknowledge the same in his presence
to be their act and deed upon the day it bears date witness my hand at office this
Ioth day of Nov. I840
                              Alex Montgomery, Clerk

State of Tennessee, Putnam County.

To Jas. W. McDaniel, Esq.
You are hereby authorized andEmpowered to take the examination of Mary A. Boyd
the femme covet Privately and apart from her Husband and relative of her free
execution of the within or annexed deed and the same so taken certify under
Putnam County Court at office the 14, day of Aug,A. D. 1857.
                        Russell Moore, Clerk

State of Tennessee, Putnam County
      Mary A. Boyd, (Fern Cobet) Having personally appeared before me and havingy
by virtueof the authoritys ma vested Examined the said Mary A. Boyd fern covet
Privately and apart from her said husband, J. W. Boyd, and she having caknowl-
edged the due Execution of the within or annexed deed freely, voluntarily and
without compulsion, constraint or coercian by her said Husband, the same as thereß
fore certified witness my hand and seal this day 15 , of Aug, A. D. 1857.
                    J. W. McDaniel

State of Tennessee, Putnam County.
      Personally appeared before me, Russell Moore, Clerk of Putnam County
Court, Alexander Boyd and Jas. W. McDaniel subscribing witnesses to the within
foregoing deed of conveyance, who being first sworn depose and say that they are
acquainted with the bargainors and that they acknowledged the same in their
presence to be their act and deed for the purposes and thingstherein contained
which is Recorded witness myhand at office the 29th day Of Ago, A. D. In58.
                    Russell Moore, Clerk.
                    J. W. McDaniel. J. P.
                    for certificatepReg. feeI160

State Tax   28½
Clerk fee   75
 certified

        Head Quarters, Unitef States Forces,
             Provost Marshal's Office,
              Nashville, Tenn, Aug,6, 1864.

I, certify That Betsy Ann Nichols of Putnam County, Tennessee, has this ady sworn
to and subscribed the Oath Of Amnesty as prescribed in the proclamation of the
President of the United States of the 8th day of December, 1863.
              James S. Boyd,
                Provost Marshal
                Capt and Asst.

Mrs. Davey Nichols original owner of records,

July, 17, 1854

Cumberland Mountain White County, Tenn
                Dera Reese
Ireceived a few lines from you a fewdays ago which gave me great satisfaction to
here from you all once more as it has bin a long time since I hard from any of you
your letter found me in as good health as could be expected from my age
You wrote that you would come out this fall and seeme I want you to do so
wothout fail health is Very good on the Mountain at present and I think if you
will come you will want to stay all the time give my respects to all of the
connection and tell them that some of them might come and see meI hope ypu will
not forget your promise so I will close. when you write direct your letters to
ClaynVille White County Tenn
                        Bashaba Mires
                        To Malinda Jared

To
    Miss Malinda Jared
            Byrns Po
            Jackson Co
            Tenn

COPIED FROM AN OLD SCHOOL LEDGER IN POSSESSION OF MRS. DAVE HIGH,
COOKEVILLE, TENN. OCT. 1857.

I. Boyd, Jef Boyd, I. Hawes, J. Jared, J. Ament, J. Holliday, W. Ensor, T. Holliday, T. Smith, D. Malone, W. Leftwich, G. Maddux, Arichet, Baler, R. E. Fain, C. Raulston, S. R. Jared, J. Garland, J. James, M. Harvey.
The free School in the 11th District, Putnam County Taught at Pleasant Grove camp Ground closed it Session Nov, 13th 1857. Session three months. Branches taught During the Session Spelling, Reafing, Arithmetic & English Grammer. Average attendance of Students 29½. Price for teaching $20 per month. Amount expended $60, $56 of the Free School fune, $4.00 from subscription.
J. Jared.
John Boyd, John Ament, John Hawes. R. Jared L. J. Boyd, Vance Malone, Woodson Yates, David Nichols, George Maddux, William Leftwich, James Carland, William Johnson, R. E. Fain, E. Dunnivan, Dow Yates, John Jared, I. Boyd, I Ament, J. Hawes, S. R. Jared, L. J. Boyd, G. Malone, W. Yates, D. N chols, G. Maddux, W. Leftwich, J. Carlen, W. J hnson, R. E. FAin, E. Dunnivan, J. Jared, A. K. Kerr, Dow Yates, J. Evans.
January, 1858.
John Boyd, John Ament, John Hawes, S. R. Jared, T. J. Boyd, G. Malone, W. Yates D. Nichols, G. Maddux, W. Leftwich, J. Carland, W. Johnson, R. E. FAin, C. Dunk van, J. Jared, A. F. Kerr, Dow Yates, J. Evans, J. Boyd, J. Ament, S. A. Jared T. J. Boyd, Y. Malone, W. Yates, J. Evans, J. Ament.
The School at Pleasant Grove camp Ground closed Feb, 5th, 1858. Session 2 months. Branches taught during the session, Spelling, reading, writing, Geography, Arithmetic & English Grammer, Average daily attendance of Students 24. Price for teaching $100 per Scholar for each month. Whole amount for the session $49.75 State of Tennessee, Putnam county, District, No 11, This Feb. 5th, 1858.

July L859.
J. Plunket, V. R. Scott, C. F. Butler, C. F. Burton, G. Evans, J. Evans, J. Denny, G. J? Maddux, C. R. Ford, J. Herbert, W. Stokes, R. W. McDowell, J. A. Huddleston, J. Pulliam, J. Fletcher, E. Evans, J. Newmand, M. Apple, O. Apple, A. Burton, E. Benson,

Aug. 1859
J. Plunket, R. Scott, C. F. Burton, G. Evans, J. Evans, J. Denny, G. J. Maddux, C. L. Ford, J. Herbert, W. Stokes, R. W. McDowell, J. A. Huddlest on, J. Pullum, J. Fletcher, E. Evans, J. Newman, M. Apple, O. Apple, A. Burton, E. Benson, A. Matthews, B. Scudder, S. Benson, W. Johnson, J. Jared,

Sept. 1859
J. Plunket, R. Scott, C. F. Burton, T. Evans, J. Evans, J. Denny, J. G. Maddux, C. R. Ford, J. Herbert, W. Stokes, R. W. McDowell, J. T Huddleston, J. Pullum, J. Fletcher, E. Evans, J. Newman, M. Apple, O. Apple, A. Burton, E. Benson, Buffalo Valley, A. Matthews, B. Scudder, S. Benson, W. Johnson, J. Jared, H. Whitehead,

Oct, 1859
J. Plunket, C. F. Burton, T. Evans, J. Evans, T. J. Maddux, J. Newman, S. E. H Huddleston, S. J. Denny, A. Burton, M. Scudder, R. Scott, J. Pullum,

Nov. 1859
J. Plunket, C. F. Burton, E. J. Newman, T. J. Maddux, J. Evans, T. Evans, J. Denny, J. E. Huddleson, J. Pullum, M. Scudder, A. B rton,
The free School closed at Rockey Springs, Nov, 16th, 1859. Session four month Branches taught during the School, Geography, reading, writing, Orthography, Arithmetic, English Grammer. Average daily attendance of Students 24, Price for teaching $25.00 per month, amount of public Money expenses $100,00, Dis,11, Putnam county, Tenn,   John Jared,

OLD SCHOOL LEDGER (CON)

J. Y. McKee, S. Maddux, W. Canard, L. Leftwich, J. H. Yoing, J. Jared, S. Camm
son, E. Cornwell G. Austin, H. Maddux, E. Dunnivan, V. Spery, L. Young, H. Oaks
Jo. Ballard, W. Gleaves C. Young, F. Berk, E. Parched, D. Souger, Jos. Overall,
J. Maxwell, C. Rogers, A. R. Lowe, A. Cameron, Foex, R. Young, J. McKee S. Maddu
J. H. Young, G. H. Maddux, S. Cameron, E. Cornwell, G. Austin, Prichet,

September,

J. Crowell, J. Maddux, C. Fox, J. G. McKee, S. Maddux, W. Chanard, J. H. Young
J. Jared , S. Cameron E. Dunnivan, V. Spivey, L. Young, A. R. Lane, H. Oaks,
Wl Gleaves. D. Sawyer, L. Loftwich, Robert Young, David Cornwell, J. G. McKee,
D. Maddux, S. H. Maddux, J. Jared, G. Austin, E. Dunnivan. F. Berk, J. Ballard
Marley Young,

October,

J. G. McKee, S. H. Maddux, W. Chanard, J. Jared, E. Dunnivan, V. Spivy. S. Camm
eron, J. Ballared, H. R. Lowe, J. H. Yoing, S. H. Maddux, L. Leftwich, V. Spivy
W. Chanard, E. Dunnivan.

November,

J. G. McKee, J. H. Maddux, S. Maddux, W. Chanard, J. Jared, E. Dunnivan, J. Ba
llard, W. Leftwich, Marley Young, John Jared,

December,

F. Berk, G. Austin, J. G. McKee, S. H. maddux, S. Maddux, John Jones, E. Dunnivan, L. Leftwich, Marley Young,

The Common School at Wesleys Chapel District No Eleven closed its Session,
Dec. 1860 Session five months, Branches taught during the School, Reading,
Writing, Geography, Arithmetic and English Grammer. Average Daily attendance
of Students . Price for teaching $25.00 per month , Amount of public money
expences$ 100 District No 11, Putnam County, Tenn,

John Jared.

J. W. McDowell, J. Jared, D. Nichols, L. Gentry, J. E. Young, P. Young, E. J.
Boyd, B. B. Jared, C. Reeves, I. Boyd, P. McCallahan, V. Spivy, J. Maxwell.
R. Jentry, W. Jentry, A. Ballard, F. Austin, C. Brasel, J. H. Cullom, Marley
Young, J. W. McDanial, J. Jared, D. Nichols, S. Gentry, J. H. Young, P. Young,
E. J. Boyd, B. B. Jared, C. R. ogers, A. Boyd, P. McCullough, V. Spivy, J. Maxi
well, W. Gentry, C. Grace, Silas. Gentry, J. H. Young, C. Brasel, Dallas Byrne
P. McCallahan, B. B. Jarod,
The Common School on Indian Creek closed its Session Sept. 5th 1862. Session
two and a half months. Branches taught during sesion , Reading, Writing, Geogr
aphy, Arithmetic and English Grammer. Average Daily attendance of Students
Prices for teaching $25.00 per month, District No 11 Putnam County.

PROPERTY OF BOB PEARSON

This Indenture made this fifth day of March one thousand eight hundred
and thirty two By and Between John Ramsey of the State of Tennessee and
County of Jackson of the oned part and William Shelton of the State and
County aforesaid of the other part witnessed that for an in consideration
of the sum of one hundred and fifty dollars to me in hand paid By the said
William Shelton- the Receipt whereof is thereby acknowledged and therewith satisfied and content I have this day Bargined and sold and
conveyed unto the Said William Shelton a certain tract or parcel of Land
containing fifty acres by survey Be the same above or less- Situated
lying and being in the County aforesaid & on the Waters of Blackburns
fork of Roarong River Butted and Bounded as follows - Viz- Beginning at
a post oak running South one hundred and Twenty five poles to a post
osk and hickory thence North one hundred and Twenty five poles to a
post oak thence East twenty four poles to the beginning encluding the
sd. Ramsey Dwelling house and the place foramely occupied by Randolph
ramsey with a part of the Said Ramsey Improvment- with the hereditions
and assetainances to have and to hold the said tract or parcel of Land and
above Described premises with its assertainces to the said William
Shelton and his heirs for ever- I hereby Bind myself my heirs and
Executors Jointly and severally to warrant & forever defend the same
from all and every person blaming the I am from all and Every person
blaming the I am on any part thereof in witness whereof I have here
unto set my hand this day and date above written in presence of us the
Two Subscribing, His mark/ John Ramsey(Seal)
Test- Thomas Nicholas, John Nicholas.

State of Tennessee, Jackson County, Pearsonally appeared before John
S. Turner Clerk of the Court Pleas and Quarter sessions for said County
John Nicholas subscribing witness to the within deed who being first sworn
deapose and say that he is acquainted with John Ramsey the Bargonar and
that he acknowledged the mentained of the same in his presence at be
his act and Deed for the purpose therein contained upon the Day it
Bears date Witness my hand at office this 15th-1834,December J.S.Turner(clk)
John Ramsey, Deed to William Shelton, 50 acres Registered in Book D,
Page 531- Registration 1,2½
State of Tennessee, Jackson County, August session 1835, Deed of Conveyance
from John Ramsey to William Shelton Deed of conveyance for fifty acres
of land lying in Jackson County was intered in Court and the execution
thereof fully proven by the Oath of Thomas Nicholas and the same is or
deced to be certified for Registration. J.S.Turner- Clk.

State of Tennessee, Jackson County, Registers office, September 15, 1835.
I Leroy B. Little Register of said County do hereby certify that the
within foregoing deed to gather with sint several Certificates is duly
Registered in my office Book D, page 531. LeRoy B. Little Register of
Jackson County.

Dec 14th 1827, No. 6919.
The State of Tennessee, To whom these Presents Shall Come- Greeting-
Know Ye, that in consideration of the sum of one per cent an paid into
the office of the Entry taken of Jackson County and entered on the 1th
day of January 1826 presentment to the provision and act of the General
Assembly of said State, passed on the Twenty second day of November one
Thousand eight hundred and twenty three and the acts empannelled thereunto
by no. 698, This is granted by the Said State of Tennessee unto Arnol Fisk.

BOB PEARSONS RECORDS CONTINUED

A certain Tract or parcel of Land containing One hundred acres by survey
bearing date the 10th day of November 1828 lying in said County and bounded
as follows to wit: Beginning at the center of what is called Moses Fisk
Turnpike road in the North boundry line of a three hundred and twenty
one tract entered in the name of Sarah Perry Fisk running thence East
fifty poles to two black jacks Thence were crossing said tract at 74
poles in all one hundred poles to a black jack, thence South one hundred
and sixty poles to a black Jack, thence East fifty poles to the beginning.

With the hereditaments and appurtances to Have and to Hold the said Tract
or Parcel of Land, with its appurtances to the said Amul Fisk and his
Heirs forever.

In witness whereof McCarroll, Governor of the State of Tennessee hath
hereunto set his hand and caused the Great Seal of the State to be affixed
at Nashville, on the 24th day of Sept. in the year of our Lord one thousand
eight hundred and Twenty, sworn and of independence of the United States
the fifty second, BY THE GOVERNOR . Daniel Graham, Secretary
Registered office Nashville Feb. 14th 1854. The within a true Copy from
the Record of my office Record in Book No. 8, witness my hand at office
Moses M.Gwan (Reg) Middle Tenn.
Copy of Grant No. 6919 Jackson County 100 acres Amel Fisk.

State of Tennessee No. 22434- To all to whom these presents shall come
Greeting: Know Ye that By Virtue of part og certificate No.571 dated the
23 day of July 1812 passed by the commissioners for West Tennessee to
Narcissa Hays for 27 acres and entered on the 9th day of November 1814
by No.3366
A Certain tract or parcel of Land containing Ten acres by survey bearing
date the 14th day of April 1815 lying in the ThirdDistrict in Jackson
County on the waters of Roaring river and bounded as follows to wit:
Beginning at a black jack and post oak about 65 yds North east of the spring
by the said Phillips running South about 60 poles to a stake and two
black jack pointers thence West fifty p. thence sixty eight and a third
poles ti a spanish oak thence East to a Chestnut tree thence thirty poles
to the beginning including the place of the said Phil lives.
With the hereditaments and appurtances to have and to hold said tract
or parcel of Land with its appurtances to the Said Phillips and his heirs
forever in witness whereof William Carroll, Governor of Tennessee hath
hereunto set his hand and caused the Great Seal of the State to be affixed
at Murfreesborough, on the 8th day of September in the year of our Lord
one thousand eight hundred and twenty four and of the Independence of
the United State the forty-nine, By the Governor, Daniel Graham Secretary
Recorded in the Registers office of West Tenn. Oct. 26, 1824.
Wm. Garock Register of West Tennessee By Alel Mc Garock DK.

DeKalb Co. Mo. Dec. 27 1860
Mr. Joe Pearson- Dear Sir your letter containing a check for $1400.00
has been recd & you can retain this as a receipt for the same
A.H.Owens Susan S. Owen, You remember in you letter that when I acknowled
the receipt of the check you would write and inform me all about my claims
against the Estate of Isaac Clark deced, If there is any more coming to me
except the above receipted you will please forward & forthwith as the times
are distressingly close as it regard money - we are as a general thing in

a state almost bording on distress. we have had foar bad crop years in seccession but the last was almost a complate failure- the present is bad enough but we dread to think of the future almost everything of the Stock kind have been sold out of the country and the counrty wi 1 have nothing to sell The next year- This with the great Political troubles does make the prospect of the future gloomy beyoun description- We here are for the Union provided we can keep togather on Hohorable terms If the threving Northern States will surrender up our Negros they have stolen and attend to their own bususness and let us attend to ours we are for the Union but if the law undermining and Ungodly acts of "obery as'd Kep up we choose honorable recession to cowardly Submission, You know how it is with rusty form about writting, I have no legal excuse but will ask you to forgive the seemingly negligance for my long silence, As it Regards the health of the Country it is good All your friends are well & all join me in sending our best w ishes to you and all enquiring friends, We will be pleased to have a letter from you or any other friends in the Land of Old Tennessee, Respectfully Your brother & Sister A.H.Owen, Susan S.Owen.

ENVELOPE;
Postmark.
Cameron Mo.
Dec. 27,

Mr. Joseph Pearson
Putnam County
Cookeville, post off.
Tenn.

PROPERTY OWNED BY BOB PEARSON HILLHAM ROAD COOKEVILLE TENN.

This indenture made the 31st day of January in the year of our Lord 1831 By and between John Petress of the County of Overton in State of Tennessee of the one part & Thomas Shoat of the County of Jackson and State afore said of the other part witness that the said John Patress for and in consideration of the sum of sixty Dollars to heir in hand paid by the said Thomas Shoat the Recept of the same is here by fully acknowledged hath and by their presents doth give grant bargin sell alien enfe off. convey & confirm into the said Thomas Shoat and his heir Executiors admistrtabors a certain tract or parcel of land lying and being in the County of Jackson State of Tennessee on the waters of Blackburns Creek aprnt of the Roaring River and bounded as follows to wit beginning at a chestnut twelve poles North of a blacj oak and post oak marked as Pointers South of a path leading from Phillips Pys to James Terrys running thence South one hundred and twenty fice poles to a black jacj thence west sixty four poles tia Hickory thence East sixty four Poles to two Hickorys thence East sixty four poles to the beginning containing fifty acres be the same more or less it being a tract of land Granted by the State of Tennessee unto the said John Patress by Grant No 3968 Dated 11th day of September 1826 the said John Patress for his self and his heirs Executors and administrators that the before Recited land and bargained Premises that he will warrant and forever defedn free from all persons or manner of persons what scsver claiming the same or any

Part thereof but to the only proper use of Heirs the said Thomas Shoat
ans his Heirs for ever in witness where of the said John Patross hath
Here on to set his Hand and affix his Seal the Day and year first Written in
the Presents of Test- John Oliver William R. Savage, John Patross (Seal)
John Patross Deed to Thomas Shoat 50 acres Land.

RECORDSOWED BY BOB PEARSON HILLIAM ROAD COOKEVILLE TENN. R#1.

The State of Tennessee No.11688- To all to whom these shall come—— Gerrting
Know Ye, That by virtue of entry No.46 Made in the office of the
Entry Taker of Putnam County and entered on the 3rd day of September
1855, pursuant to the provisions of an act of the General Assembly
said State passed on the 9th day of Januarym 1830. There is Granted by
the said State of Tennessee unto Joseph Pearson, a certain tract or
parcel of land containing Eighteen Acres by survey, bearing date the
Sixth day of June 1856, lying in the said county of Putnam on the water
of Blackburns Fork beginning on a Post Oak and Post Oak and black Jack
pointers convey of a one hundred acres track belonning to said Pearson
Running West Eighteen poles to a Stake on the time of a Three hundred
and twenty acres tract that said Pearson lives on now with the East
boundry line of the same one hundred and sixty poles to two post okes
and pointers cover of the same on the west side of the Road leading
from White Plains to Terrys East crossing said road at two poles
crossing the Cookeville Road at Eighteen poles to a Black Jack on the
East side of the Road covers to the one hundred acre tract. South with
the West boundry line of said one hundred acre tract one hundred and
sixty poles to the beginning. with the hereditaments and appurtances
to have and to hold the said Tract or parcel of land with its appurtances to the said Joseph Pearson and his heirs forever.
In witness whereof Andrew Johnson, Governor of the State of Tennessee, h
hath hereunto set his Hand and caused the Great Seal of the S ate to
be affixed at Nashville, one the 10th day of July in the year of our
Lord One thousand Eight Hundred and fifty six. and of the independence
ofthe United States the Eightyth Year, By the Governor Andrew Johnson
L.M.Buvtord Secetary.
Joseph Pearson is entitled to the within described Tract of Land
John T. Day Register of the mountain district Recorded on the Registers
office for the mountain District on Book No 10 Page 751, John T. Day
Register of the Mountain District.
Grant No.11688 Joseph Pearson 18 acres Putnam County 1st July, 1856

State of Tennessee No. 1842.
To all to whom these presents shall come—Greeting: Know Ye that for
and in consideration of the sum of one cent pe acre, paid into the
office of the Entry Taker of Kackson Countym and entered on the 9th
day of January 1826, pursuant to the provisions of an act of the General
assembly of said State, passed on the third day of December one thousand
eight hundred and twenty five by No. 715 there is granted by thhe said
State of Tennessee unto Tho as M.Aholas—A certain tract or parcel of
land containing one hundred acres by survey beraing date the 16th day
of Feburary 1829 lying in said county on the waters of Blackburns fork
of Roaring iver and bounded as follows. Beginning at a Black Oak North
of a field occupied by Isaac Richmonds, Running North one hundred and sixty

poles to a small post oak and Hickory Thence west one hundred poles to two
dogwoods in the part boundry line of James Terry 's 640 acres Tract, Thence
South with said line one hundred and sixty poles to two small chestnuts
Thence East one hundred poles to the Beginning including Austin Shoats
improvments. With the hereditaments and appertances. To have and to hold
the said tract or parcel of land with its appertances to the said Thomas
Nicholas, and his heirs forever, in witness where of William Carroll,
Governor of the State of Tennessee, has hereunto set his hand and caused the
great seal of the state to be affixed at Nashville on the 9th day of August
in the year of Our Lord One thousand eight hundred and thirty and of the Inde
pendance of the United States the fifty fifty. By the Governor Wm. Carroll
Daniel Cooham Secretaty. Thomas Nicholas is entitled to the within
described land R. Nelson Register of Mountain District. Recorded in my
office Book C. page 533 R. Nelson Register of the mountain District.
No. 1842 Thomas Nicholas 100 acres Jackson County.

State of Tennessee NO. 4279 - To all to Whom these Presents shall come
Greeting: Kno you that by virtue of entry N537 made in the office of
the entry taker of Jackson County and entered on the 8th day of January
1830 pursuant to the provisions of an act of the General Assembly of said
State passed on the 3rd day of December 1825. there os Granted by the said
State f Tennessee unto William Shelton assigned of John Ramsey a certain
tract or parcel of land containing three hundred acres by survey bearing
date the 2day of March 1832 lying in said County on the waters of Blackburns fork of Roaring River Beginning at a black oak Wear of improvements n
now occupied by Rand ph Ramsey running East Two Hundred and two poles
to a Black Oak and post oak on the Old Collins River tract: Thence North
passing the South west Corner of Jess KayKendall's fifty acre tract at
fifty eight poles in all with said line One hundred and fifty poles to a
Hickory the North West corner of said tract, Thence East with the North
boundry line of said tract thirty nine poles to two blackjacks and a
hickory in said line, thence North one hundred and fifty two and one fourth
poles to two small post oaks thence west with the South boundry line of
John Petross fifty acre tract passing his South West corner at Ninty eight
poles in all one hundred and twenty four poles to a black oak, in the East
boubdry line of Jess Kuykendall one hundred acre tract, Thence South with
said line twenty six and one fourth poles to a chestnut the South East
corner of said tract thence West Eighteen poles to a post oak in said
corner of Thomas Nicholas North East corner of his one hundred acres,
Thence South with the Easr boundry line of said tract one hundred and
sixty poles to a black oak the South East corner of said tract, Thence West
with the South boundry line of said tract one hundred poles to a chestnut
tree the South West corner of said tract, Thence South one hundred and
sixteen poles to the beginning.
With the hereditamants and appurtances, to have and to hold the said tract
or parcel of land with its appurtances to the said William Shelton and his
heirs forever. In witness whereof Newton Cannon, Governor of the State of
Tennessee has here unto set his hand and caused the great seal of the State
to be affixed at Nashville on the 22n d of January 1836 and Year of our
Independence By the Governor N. Cannon Luke Lee Secetary.
William Shelton is entitled to the within described land T.R.Nelson Register
of the mountain District.
No. 4379 William Shelton assignee of John Ramsey 300 acres Jackson County
To be left at Major Richard F. Cook's in Jackson County with request for
him to have it delivered to the owner - Register.

PROPERTY OWNED BY BOB PEARSON HILLHAM ROAD COOKEVILLE TENN.

State of Tennessee No 800- To all to whom these presents shall come
Greeting, Know ye that for and in consideration for the sum of one cent per
acre paid into the office of the Entry Taker of Jackson County and entered
on the 8th day of Feburaru 1826, pursuant to the provisions of one act
of the General assembly of said State passed on the third day of December
one thousand Eight hundred and twenty-five by No 874 then Geanted by the
said State of Tennessee unto Mathewv Kuykendall a certain tract or parcel
of land containing fifty acres by survey bearing date the 8th day of May
1827 lying in said County on the Waters of Thomas Nicholas Mill Creek and
bounded as follows Beginning at a hickory thence West Eighty nine poles
to a post oak- thence North ninty poles to two hickories, Thence East
Eighty nine poles to the beginning with the hereditaments and appurtendances to have and to hold the said Tract or parcel of land withits
appurtendances to the said Matthew Kuykendall and his heirs forever, In wit
ness whereof Sam Huston Governor of the State of Tennessee hath hereunto
set his hand and caused the Great Seal of the State to be affixed at
Nashville on the 10t h day of the Independence of the United States the
fifty third, By the Governor Sam Huston, Daniel Graham Secretary,
Matthew Kuykendall 50 acres Jackson County Recorded in mu office Book B
page 232 R. Nelson Register of the Mountain District.

State of Tennessee Jackson County- This day came John Dowell before me
John Terry a Justice of the peace for said County & made oath in due form
of law that a certain note of hand Executed from Joseph Pearson to him
for one hundred and six dollars Sometime in December 1851 is lost or
unintentionally mislaid or the possessions of the same has been filon-
iously obtained by Irme Pearson & that he has not sold Bartered transfered
assigned or aonveyed by him self or by any Person for him said note, This
16th day of November 1853. Sworned to & subscribed before me the date
above John Terry J.P. John Dowell .

State of Tennessee, No 3670- To all to whom these presents shall come
Greeting: Know Ye that by virtue of Entry No 1666 made in this office of
the enrty taker of Jackson County and entered on the 30th day of December
1830 pursuant to the provisions of act of the General Assembly of said
State passed on the 9 h day of January 1830 thence Granted by the said
State of Tennessee unto Thomas Choate a certain tract or parcel of land
containing fifty acres by survey bearing date the thday of march 1830
lying in the Said County on the Waters of Blackburns fork of Roaring River
Beginning at a small Black Oak the South East corner of said Choates
original fifty acre tract running East with John Raineys North boundry
line of his three hundred acre tract passing his North east corner at
thirty two poles in all sixty four poles to three black jacks, thence
thence North one hundred and twenty five poles to three chestnuts, thence
West sixty four poles to a chestnut the North East corner of said original
fifty acres tract thence South one hundred and twenty five poles to the
beginning. With the hereditaments and appurtnedances to have and to hold
the said tract or parcel of land with its appurtendances to the said Thomas
Choate and his heirs forever. In witness whereof William Carroll Governor
of the State of Tennessee had hereunto set his hand and caused the Great
Seal of the State to be affixed at Nashville on the 3rd day of February
1835 and 59 years. By the Governor Wm Carroll, F.G.Keith Secretary.
Recorded in my office Book E. page 409 M. Nelson Register of the mountain
District.
No.3670 Thomas Choate 50 acres Jackson County, Thomas Choate is intitled
to the within discribed land R. Nelson Register of the mountain District.

BOB PEARSON'S RECORDS CONTINUED

This Indenture made this third day of January in the year of Our Lord
Eighteen hundred and thirty four Between Mathew Kuykendall of the
County of Jackson and state of Tennessee of the one part and William
Shelton of the State and County aforesaid of the other Part witness
that for an inconsideration of the sum of forty dollars to him in hand
Paid by said Shelton the Receipt whereof is hereby acknowledged hath
this Shelton a certain tract or parcel of land situated as follows
Viz) lying and baing in the said County of Jackson and state aforesaid
on the waters of Thomas Nicholas mill creek supposed to be the Waters
of Bear Creek and bounded as follows. Beginning at a Hickory running
south ninty poles to a hickory thence West Eighty poles to two hickories
thence East eighty nine poles to the beginning with the hereditaments
and appurtendances to have and to hold the said tract or parcel of land
with the appertances to the said William Shelton and his heirs forever
and containing in all fifty acres and do bind myself my heirs Executors
Adminstrators to warrant and forever defend from me and my heirs in
witness whereof I have here unto set my hand and seal this day and date
first above mentioned. Matthew Kuykendall (Seal) Peter Kuykendall
Curtis Terry,
State of Tennessee, Jackson County. Pearsonally appeared before me
William Scarland clerk of the Court of Pleas & Quartly session for said
claim by Matthew Kuykendall and acknowledged that he executed the within
Deed of conveyance for the purposes therein contained, witness my hand
at office this 10th Nov. 1834, William Scarland(Clk).
This Indenture made this Day of January in the year of Our Lord Eighteen
& Thirty four between Mathew Kuykendall of the one Part and William
Shelton of the other Part.
State of Tennessee , Jackson County, Registers office Jan. 21, 1835
I Leroy B. Settle Register of said County of Jackson do hereby Certify
that the within & foregoing deed of Conveyance together with the Clerks
Certificate is duly registered in my office Book D. & page 517.
Le Roy B. Settle Register of Jackson County.

State of Tennessee — No 3968   To all to whom these presents shall
come————Greeting: Know Ye, That for and in consideration of the sum
of Twelve and one half cents per acre paid into the office of the Entry
Taker of Jackson County and entered on the Twelth day of July, 1842
pursuant to the provisions of all Act of the General Assembly of said
State passed on the 22 day of November one thousand eight hundred and
twenty three by No 399. There id granted by the said State of Tennessee
unto John Patross a certain Tract or Parcel of Land containing fifty
Acres by survey bearing date the 30th day of Aughst 1825 lying in said
County on the waters of Blackburns fork of Roaring River and bounded
as follows to wit: Beginning at a Chestnut twelve poles North of a
black oak and post oak marked as pointers South of a path leading from
Phillips Phys to James Terry's Running thence South one hundred and
twenty five poles to a Black Jack thence West Sixty four poles to a
hickory, Thence North one hundred and twenty five poles to two hickories
thence East Sixty four poles to the beginning including the house and
improvements last occupied by Mathew Patross.

With the hereditaments and appertenances To have and to Hold the said
Tract or Parcel of Land with its appertenances to the said John Patross
and his heirs forever. In witness whereof William Carroll Governor
of the State of Tennessee hath hereunto set his hand and caused the great
Seal of the State to be affixed at Nashville on the Eleventh day of
September- In the year of our Lord One thousand eight hundred and twenty
six and of the Independence of the United States the fifty first.
By the Governor Wm. Carroll, Daniel Graham Sectrary.
Recorded in the Registers office of West Tennessee Febryary 28" Stith
Harrison DK. John Patross is entitled to the within mentioned tract
of land T.M.Garack D. Register of West Tennessee.
No. 3968 John Patross 50 acres Jackson County.

Know all men by these presents that I Thomas Choate have this day bargained
and sold and do hereby transfer and convey to Joseph Pearson and his
heirs for ever for the consideration of Thirty five Dollars to me paid
two tracts of Land in the State of Tennessee, Putnam County and district
No 3 on the waters of Blackburns fork containing by estimantion one
hundred acres be the same more or less and bounded as follows;
1st Tract Beginning at a chestnut twelve poles north of a Black oak&post
oak marked as pointers South of a path leading from Phillips Phy to Jmaes
Terry 's running thence South one hundred and twenty five poles to a
Black Jack thence North one hundred and twenty five poles to two hickories
thence East Sixty four poles to the beginning containing fifty acres by Grant
No. 3968 Dated 11th day of September 1826.
2nd Tract Begining at a small Oak the South East corner of said Choate
original fifty acre tract running East with John Ramseys North boundry
line of his three hundred acre tract passing his North east corner at thirty
two poles in all sixty four poles to three Black Jacks thence North one
Hundred and twenty five poles to three chestnuts thence West sixty four
poles to a chestnut the North East corner of said original fifty acres
tract thence South one hundred and twenty five poles to the beginning
containing fifty acres by Grant 189 3670 Dated 3rd day of February 1825
To have and to hold the same ti the said Joseph Pearson his heirs and assign
foe ever do convenant withthe said Pearson that I am lawfully seized of
said land have a good rite to convey it and that the same is incumbered, I
do further convenant and bind myself my heirs and Representaves to warrant
and forever defend the title to the said land and every part thereof th the
said Pearson his heirs and assigns aganist the lawful claims of all persons
whatever This 25th day of February 1843, Thomas Choate.
Attest J.M.Goodbar J.L.H.Huddleston.
Thomas Choate to Deed Joseph Pearson 100 acres.

PERSONAL LETTER;

Joseph Pearson, Sir late last evening I understood that Isaac Buck was
going to start to Nashville I wish to send by him for some books for the use
of my office as this county have hereto fore been in dispute- The County
Court Authorized me to get Books and they would then pay me* I wish to get
$25.00 and if I can get the same or less amount please send me a few lines,
by the bearer of this and I will be at your house- and give note & security
if you want security and pay the same Back at the time the other note is due
with 12½ cts Interest thereon I would have to come this morning more than a
man came to my house late last Evening and is wanting some buisness done
in the office, Yours in haste W.H.Carr

I joseph Pearson bind myself to pay Josiah Phy the sum of Six hundred
Dollars the consideration of this obligation in such that whereas the said
Josiah Phy has this day purchased of me for Three hundred Dollars on the
following payments to wit: one hundred Dollars to be paid the first day
of June 1853 and one hundred the first day of June 1854 and the 3rd hundred
the first day of June 1855 For which his notes under seal have this day
him executed to me barring interest from the dates Five tracts of land
in Jackson County in District No.10 State of Tennessee Bounded as follows
Begining by estimanton fifty acres Beginning at a post oak marked with
H.T. Running west one hundred poles to a small Hickory, Thence South Eighty
poles to a small Hickory & Black oak, Thence East one hundred poles to a
stake in the Barnes, Thence North Eighty Poles to the Beginning including
Sume Springs about 17 as miles from Phillip Phy as staked in location
the second tract containing by estimantion fifty acres beginning at a
Hickory twenty five poles East of Nicholas North West corner of his orifinal
survey running North one hundred poles to a black oak thence East eighty
poles to a black walnut, Thence South one hundred poles to a stake in said
Nicholas North boundry line of said fifty acre survey Thence West Eighty
poles to the beginning the 3rd tract containing fifty artes beginning at a
Hickory the North West corner of the said Nicholas Fifty Acre tract running
North Forty Poles to the two Hickories, Thence West Eighty Poles to a post
oak & Hickorys in the North boundre line of said fifty acre tract, Thence
North with said line sixty Poles to the begining Also one other tract containing fifty eight & half acres lying near the said discribed tracts od land.
conveyed by Thomas Choate to William Carr Also o ne other tract containing
twelve acres more or less lying adjoining the last mentioned tract of land
Now if I shall makek or cause to be made to the said Josiah Phy his heirs
or assigns a good and sufficient title in fee simple with general warrantly
to said tracts of land on the making of the last payment. Then this obligation to be void, this 1st day of June 1852. Joseph Pearson (Seal)
Attest John Terry Wm. A. Terry,

This indenture made this sixth day of January one thousand Eight Hundred
and Thirty eight between Thomas Nicholas of White County and State of Tenn
essee of tje one part and Nathan W. Wallace of the County and State aforesaid
of the other part witness that whereas the said Nicholas hath Bargained
and solf unto the saod Wallace a certain tract or parcel of la nd containing
one hundred acres being the same more or less lying in Jackson County
on the waters og Blackburns fork of Roaring River and bounded as Follows:
Beginning at a Black oak North of a field occupied by Isaac Richard running
North one hundred and sixty poles to a small post oak and hickory thence west
one hundred poles to two Dogwoods in the east Boundry line of James Terry
six hundred and Forty acre tract thence South with said line one hundred
and sixty poles to two small chestnuts thence east one hundred poles to the
Beginning with the hereditaments and appertenimaces to have and to hold
the aforesaid tract or parcel of land free from any claims either by me
or my heris forever in Testimony where the said Nicholas hath hereunto
set his hand and seal the date first above mentioned, Thomas Nicholas (Seal
Attest John Welsh Hugh G. Huddleston
Thomas Nicholas Deed to Mathew H. Wallace 100 acres.

State of Arkansas, Carroll County, Sept 13th A.D. 1854.
Dear Mother, Brother & Sister, It is in and through the kind mercies of
our ~~~~~~~ Creator that we are in Telerable Health that is they are all
well Except Bad Colds with out it is myself I am not well altogether

PERSONAL LETTER CONTINUED

I am teaching school at this time But we hope and pray that these few lines
will find you all well at there arrival we have nothing very strange to
ritee to you only I received your letter on yesterday
which give us great Satisfaction to hear that you was all well and I was
truly glad to hear that Mother was living with you we have been looking
with longing anixety for the news which have just arrived Our calculation
is to come as soon as posable that sion & myself) If no providen trial
him derence one or both of us will be there as soon as possible that is
this fall and we are comming to fetch mother home with hs and to see Justice
nowhere without any regard to Tom old Jake or any whom may consider themselves conserned on the stipe Tribe wee want mother to be in rediness atall
times to come with us know knowing how soon wee will bee there I .F.Carter
want you I Pearson to get the Best counsel for me conserning Polly the Negro
& mothers dowery in that land in White County and wee will sell it cheap
for the cash when wee come I know old Jake sold it But no title has never
went from me yet, I have written to Wm . Cumming of VanBuren County conserning the matter and I am looking for an answer Every dau   I think I will
straten them when I come we do not want to get into deficulties with Old
Kake But so far as Tom if conserned wee do not ax him any favors whatever
he is no Body and all who know him knows that, we will come in a two horse
waggon and wee want mother to be certain and get ready and stay Reddy
untill wee come wee will be there Isaac Clark your nephew will start to
that Counrty in a few days Jejn A. Anderson will come with us so he says
give our best love to all friends wee will Bring our Letter to a close
By Subscribing our names as your Friends till Doeth may God Bless you all.
Wm. F.C. Carter & Sion .W"ife J. Pearson & wife)
Rebecca Stipe Joseph Pearson & Wife. From Berryulle Ark. Sept 20 To Joseph
Pearson White Plains P.O. Putnam County Tenn.

I Elijah Car have this day bargained and sold and do herebe transfer and
convey to Joseph Pearson and his heirs forever for the consideration of Three
hundred and forty Dollars to me paid four trasts of land in the State of
Tennessee Putnam County and District Nelst. containing by estimation
Two hundred and eight and one half acres. First tract containing fifty eight
and one half acres Beginning at a Post Oak and white oak & Pointer the North
West corner of John B. Mc Carmacks four hundred acres survey & in the East
boundry line of First entry on the North side if the Walton Roads of three
hundred and twenty acres running thence North with said East boundry line
fifty one poles to a chestnut and white oak & pointers the North East corner of said three hundred and twenty acres survey thence West thirty poles
to a postank and Pointers the North boundey line of said three hundred &
twenty acre survey, Thence North with the East boundry line if Fisk's
second Three hundred and twenty acre survey fifty eight poles to a Readoak
and Pointers in said Easr boundry line, Thence Easr supposed to be with
or neat James Peaks line Eighty Poles to a Red oak and Hickory & Pointers at
Murpheys West boundry line eighty six poles to a postoak and Read oak &
Pointers tje South West corner of said Murpheys Survey boundry line of said
survey one hundred and eighty nine Poles to a stake & Pointers Thence
South twenty three Poles to the North boundry line of aforesaid four hundred
acre survey Thence West with the North boundry line of the aforesaid four
hundred acre survey to the beginning fifty acre tract containing afifty acres.
Beginning at a Postoak Marked J.L. Running West one hundred Poles to a

small Hickory and Blackoak , Thence East one hundred Poles to a stake, Thence
North Eighty Poles to the beginning Third tract containing fifty acres Beginning at a Hickory running North one hundred Poles to a stake in the North
boundry line of the first Discribed fifty acres tract, Thence West Eighty
Poles to the beginning, Fourth tract containing fifty acres Beginning at a
Hickory the South West corner of the first mentioned fifty acre tract running
North forty Poles to two Hickorues, Thence West Eighty Poles to a Post
oak & Hickories, Thence South one hundred Poles to two Hickorises & Postoak in the west boubdry line on the first mentioned fifty acre tract
Thence North with said line sixty Poles to the beginning. To have and to
hold the same to the said Joseph Pearson his heirs and assigns forever
I do convenant with the saod Joseph Pearson that I am lawfully seixed of
said land have a good right to convey it and that the same as-unincumbered
I do further convenant and bind myself my heirs and Representatives to
warrant and forever defend the title to the said land and every part there
of th the said Joseph Pearson his heirs and assigns against the lawful
claims of all Pearso whatever This 11th day of April 1855.
Entered and delivered in our presents, This 11th day Apr. 1855,
Isaac Buck, J.M.Douglass,
State of Tennessee, Puntm County, Pearsonally appeared before me Russell
Moore Clerk of Putnam Court & Elijah Car the within bargained with
whom I am personally acquainted and who acknewledged the deed Executioner
of the within Deed of Conveyance to be his act and Deed for the purpose
and things therein contained witnessed my hand at office the 11th day of
April 1855, Russell Moore clerk, This deed was filed in my office and
dated for Registration the 24th Dec, 1857 at 7½ O'Clock P.M. in Reception
Book on pagees 54& 55 registered in Book B. on pg. 291& 92.
William Baker(Reg) of Putnam County.
Elijah Car Deed to Joseph Pearson 208½ Acres, State Tax 30 clerks fee 25.
askn. Apr. 11th 1855, Recorded on page 142 Book A. Putnam County Tenn.
R. Moore Clk. Reg. Fee $1.75 From N, J, Pearson.

I mathew H. Wallace of Jackson County and State of Tennessee nave t is day
bargained and de hereby transfer and convey to Joseph Pearson of the
County and State aforesaid his heirs and addigns forever the consideration
of the sum of four himdred dollars to me paid three certain tracts or parcels
of land in the State 8gTennesses Kackson County district No 10 the first containing by estimation one hundred and eighty nine acres be the same more or
less all said three tracts are situated on the waters of Roaring river on
Blackburns fork of roaring river the said first tract covers a fifty acre
survey which was granted to William Shelton assige of John Ramsey and from
said Ramsey by Grant No. 4379 and from said Ramsey to the said William Shelton
the saod first tract bounded as follows Beginning at a hickory two hic cries
and chestnuts Pointers it being the beginning corner of a fifty nine acre
survey more or less conveyed to the said William Shelton to Tholas Choate
running thence, East Seventy degrees South one hundred thirty two poles to a
small Hickory & small post oak a chestnut & hickory pointers in the easr boundry
line of the original tract, thence South forty two poles to two black Jacks
and a hickory the North oasr corner of Jess Kuykendall fifty acres tract, thence
West thirty nine poles to a hickory the North West corner of said Tract thence
South one hundred and thirty fore poles to a black Jack and three black Jacks
and one postoak pointers thence West fifty nine degrees North one hundred and
forty poles to a post oak & three postoaks pointers thence North twebty five
degrees West twenty two poles to a stake and four red oaks pointers in the South
boundry line of a one hundred acres tracr that I the so Mathew H. Wallace now
lives on thence Eastwardly four poles to a black oak the South East corner of
said tract thence North West to the East boundry line of said tract one hundred

and thirty poles to a post oak in said line the North east corner of
said one hundred acre tract thence East eighteen poles to a chestnut
the South east corner of said tract thence to the Beginningm the other
secind tract s pposed to be on the waters of Bear Creek & bounded as follows
Beginning at a Hickory running thence South ninty poles to a hickory thence
West Eighty nine poles to a post oak thence North ninty poles to two hickories
thence east eighty nine poles to the beginning containing fifty acres
which was c nveyed from Jess Kuykundall dec'd to the said William Shalton
by deed of conveyance from Jess Kuykendall dated the 3rd of January 1834,
the third tract or parcel of land was granted by the State of Tennessee to
Thomas Nicholas by Grant No.1842 thence from sacd Nicholas to me the said
Matthew H. Wallace by a deed of conveyance dated the sixth day of January
1838 and bounded as follows to wit: Beginning at a black oak, North of a
field oxxupped by Isaac Richards running North one hundred & sixty poles
to a S,all post oak and hickory thence West one hundred pokes to two
dogwoods in the east boundry line of James Terry 640 tract , thence south
with sd line one hundred and sixty poles to two small chestnuts thence
East one hundred poles to the Beginning, containing one hundred acres including Austin Choate improvements to have and to hold the aforeasid land
to the said Joseph Pearson his heirs and assigns forever ll do covenant
with the sacd Joseph Pearson that I am lawfully seized of saif land, have
a good right to convey it- and that the same is unincumbered- I do further
convenant and bi d myself my heirs and representaves aho warrant and forever
defend tha title to the said land and every part thereof to the said
Joseph Pearson his heirs and assigns forever against the lawful claims of
all persons whatsoever Executed and delivered in the presence of John B.
Pointer, April 6, 1841, Anderson Cole, Mathew H. Wallace (Seal)
State of Tennessee Registeres office Sept 9th, Jackson Co. I Joshua R.
Stone Register of said county herebe certify that the within & foregeing
deod of conveyance from Mathew H. Wallace to Joseph Pearson together with the
clerks certification is duly Registered in my office Book E. & page 109&110
Joshua R. Stone Register of Jackson County.
Mathew H. Wallace Deed 330 acres To Joseph Pearson bargainors Sale.
Register fec $1.50

This Indentyre made and entered into this 30th day of May 1842, between
John Anderson of County od White and State of Tennessee of the one part
and William W. Sims of the County and State aforesaid of the other part in
trust for the benefir of my securities in the debted herein after mentioned
witnesseth that whereas the said John Anderson is justly endebted to Rebecca
Anderson in the Sum of $40. due by note dated 29 Apr. 1835 and akao
indebted to the said Rebecca in the sum of Ten Dollars per anum as an
annuity during her hational life as set fourth in a covenant between the
Heirs if James Anderson a nd Deed which instrument is registered in the
Registers office of White County on the 28th Oct. 1835 in Book J. page
222 & of which now due and unpaid and where as I and justly liable and
responsible to James Anderson for $700.00 which is payable in the Branch
Pank of Tennessee at Sparta dated 19th may 1842 and due 6 months after
said note os endorsed by Preston Anderson, James Scott and John Anderson
, this note was na e for my exculsive use and benefit And whereas I am
justly endebted to Jo Pearson in the Sum of $435.40 due 6th February 1841
in which James Anderson is my Security - and whereas I am justly indebted

to the representative of George Griffireth estate in the Sum of Eighty Dollar
due 5th March 1840, in which James Anderson is my Security and whence I am
justly indebted to the Guardian to the minor heirs of William Roberts Deed
in the Sim of $15.00 dated some time in the year of 1842 in which Daniel
Sandy is my security: none of which debts have yet been suid on— And whereas
I am justly indebted to William Hill Guardian in the sum of $72.16 dated 30 Dec
1839 in which Preston Anderson my Security on which syit ins noe commended also
one other note to Isaac Taylor for $200. due some time in 1835 or 1848 in which
Warren and Debrell are my securities which is also sued on Also injudgment of
Lewis Bohannon agansit mysely andDibrell my security on a note foe $100 in
silver beofre John Pennington Wsqr and stayed ny James Anderson also a Judgement
of W. Hills and aganist my self James Anderson security for avout $100. beofre
Robert H.M.Manns Wsqr. stayed by Jo Herd— and also oneother Judgment in forever
of William B. Hall aganist myself for $50. Dollars before John Pennington
Wsqr. stayed by Solomn Wilhite. And whereas the said John Anderson being wilk
ing and desirous to some payment of all carrddebte-and-mentioned-securities
in this several liabilities— now for the purpose aforesaid the said John Anders
on makes this transfer To wit, for that portion of debts upon thisch no suit
has yet been commanded he doth granted bargained and sold and transfered to the
said W.G. Sims his Ensor. Admr. in trust the following described real and personal property To.wit. One tract of land containing 12¾ acres held by De'ed
from James Anderson and dated 11th May 1829bRegistered in Registers office
on 22 Apr. 1835, in Book J. page 201, of Said County. Also one other tract
of land containing 120 acres held by Deed from John McAwly dated 18th 1832
and Registered 29 January 1833 in Book H, Page 381 also one other land
containing 160 acres held by Deed from Joe Dennison dated 6th Sept. 1833
Registered 6th Sept. 1833 in Book H, page 508 Refered to said Registration
willifully slow. also all my ho se hold and Kitchen furnityre and framing
tools such as are not ecempt from Execution— and also my Negro slave man
named Peter a slave for life and the slaid John Anderson does hereby
convey unto William G, Sims Trustee aforestis the following described
property real and personal for the use and benefit of those debts before
mentioned exclusive which have been and upon To wit: One Tract og Land
hold by deed from Jess Bullock and wife and James Howard containing 114
acres Registered 28 Nov. 1838 in Book 8 page 145 Also one other Tract of 338
acres hold by deed from William Howard Registered 28 Oct 1834 in Book
J. Page 97 also one other tract 100 acres hold by deed from William Parker
dated 11th Dec. 1829 which Deed of registered also one half of a Tract
of Land lying on the main Caney Fork whereon Jacob Anderson Jr. now lives
conveyed by said Jacob Anderson Jr. by Deed to said Josiah Anderson by Deed
which Deed id Registered in the Aegisters office of said County, Also
2 stills and thirty Still Tubes now in the possession of Jacon Anderson Jr.
also six head of horses 2 yolk of oxen and one ox wagon, 10 heads of cattle
40 head of Hogs 7 sheep and one Negro woman named Vice a slave for live—
all of which property the saod John Anderson herebe conveys said Sims for
the purpose aforesaid and herebe warrents and binds himself to defend the
title thereof now this is the understanding that if the said John Anderson
shall will and truly pay ot cause to be paid all andevery of said debts
and judgments and shall save all his securities herein beofre mentioned
harmless and face from all less damages, then this Indenture to be null
and void and the right to said property shall revest him the said John
Andersonhis Heirs &. And in the mentioned said property bath/and/ real
and personal shall remain in rhe ahnds of said John Anderson subject to the
provision of this Indenture, But shaule the said John Anderson fail to pay
or cause to be paif the beofre described debts and Judgments and should

he suffers an execution or executions to be run aganist any one or more
of all of said securities for the collections of said debts and judgments
shall be the duty of said Trustee to take posession of so much of said
property as situated for each particular character of debts herein provided as in his Judgement will be sufficient to Satisfy the particular debt
or debts that may be then pressing of those herein contained and surrender
on the same into the hands of such officer or officers as may have the
collection of said debts or judgments that said officer may kame his
levy and sell same ordering to law ~~and his respects back~~ of the two
classes of debts herein describing to wit those that are sued and those
that are sued appropariting the property to each class in the manner here
in particularly described But should the said Anderson require the said
Trustee to sell and dispose herein he shall pursue the alw governing
Executiors sales and is execution except us to the land and regards thing
are required to be sold at the court house door in Sparta after giving 20
days public notice, This deed is not intended to debur said Anderson the
priviledge of selli g any of the above described property himself provided
he sells the same for sash price with the cnsent of the Trustee and shall
aos9 pay the proceeds thereof to that particular class of debts herein
mentioned- should the note of James Anderson of 700 payable Bank be renewed
agreeable to the rules and regulations of said Bank said note shall through
all its different renewals and it is hereby declared to have and to hold
a contranaous line on said property- untill John Anderson shall have fully
dischared and paid off the same- should said Trustee be called upon to
sell said property agreeable to this deed he shall be allowed a fair com-
penseiob for his trouble, and if a surplus should remain in his hands he shall
pay the same to the said John Anderson his heirs and Ect., And the said
William G. Sims agrees to execute this Trustee- Witness our hands and seals
this date 1st above written, Sighnd, John Anderson ack. 30 May 1842
W.G.Sims (Seal) ack. 31, 1842.
State of Tennessee, White County- Pearsonally appeared before me Nicholas
Oldham, Clerk of White County Court John Anderson/~~Clerk~~ William G. Sims
Subscribers to the acked. Deed with whom I am personally acquainted and
who both acknowledged the due axecution of the within Deed for the purpose
therein contained which is Recorded Witness my hand at office the 31st May
1842, Signed Test N. Oldham Clerk of the White County Court.
State of Tennessee, White Co nty, I hereve certify that the amount Deed from
John Anderson to William G. Sims was filed and dated in R ception Book N.1
page 3 1st of June 1842 at ¼ past 9 O clock A.M. (and) rigistered in my
office 2nd June 1842 in book N. pages 44& 45 an 46, Given at office same day
Test Oldham Deputy of R Smith Register of White County, Copy of Exhibit
A. Test R S. Rhea C.A.M. By W.E. Nelson D.C.
John Anderson Trust Deed To W1G. Sims

I curtis Terry of Jackson County and State of Tennessee and District No.10
have this day bargained and sold and do herebe transfer and conveyed to
Joseph Pearson of the County State and District of foresaid fir the consideration of the Forty Dollars to me paif the receipt acknowledged a certain tract
or parcel of land in the county state and district aforesaid it being
a part of a survey Gwanted to William Ramsey by Grant No.335of containing
by estimation one thousand acres be the same more or less one Bounded as
Follows Beginning at a stake in the ~~fest~~ fork of Bear Creek glade in the
west Boundry line of a three hundred and ten Acres survey Entered by Fisk
thence west 126 and one half poles to a Black Jack & pointers, Thence S
one hundred & twenty six and one halfpoles to a small Hickory, Thence

East one hundred twenty six and one hald poles to a stake in the west
Boundry line of "isk said survey Thence North with said west Boundry line
one hundred and twenty six & one half poles to the Beginning to have & to
hold the same to the said Joseph Pearson his heirs & assigns forever & do
covenant with the said Joseph Pearson that I am alwfully seized of said
land have a good tight to convey it & that the same in unincumbe ed I do
further bind my self my heirs & assignd, To warrant and defend the title
to the said land and convey part thereof said Joseph Pearson to his herir
& assigns forever aganist the lawful claims of all Persons what so ever
in witness whereof I the said Curtis Terry have here unto set my hand
and seal this twenty six day of November 1845. Executed & delivered in our
presents Thomas Cates, Ninson M. Terry, Curtis Terry (Seal)
State of Tennessee Pearsonally appered before me Sampson W. Cassetty clerk
of Jackson County Court Curtis Terry the bargainor to the written and fore
going deed with whom I am personally acquainted and who acknowledged the
same to be this act and deed for the purposes therein expresed witnessed my
hand at office this 6th day o f March 1848. S.W.Cassetty(Clk) March.
State o Tennessee Jackson Co. Refistered of Jackson County do hereby
certify that tha with in deed from Curtis Terry to Joseph Pearson to gether
with the clerks entrys Registeres in my office in Book G. Page 426,
John M. Gipson Reg. of Jackson County.

State of Tennessee Jackson County, Pearsonally appeared before me Sampson
W. Cassetty clerk of Jackson County Court, John Harris the barginer of the
within deed with who I am personally acquainted who being duly sworn
acknowledged the within deed to be his act and deed for the purposes therein
contained witness my hand at office this 26th day of January 1853,
S.W.Cassetty Clk.

State of Tennessee Jacksnon County, Registers office thus 3rd day of
Oct. 1853 at 2 Oclock P.M. I John M. Gipson di herebe certify that the
within Deed from John Harris to John M. Carlton together with the clerks
certificate thereto is duly Registered in my office in Registers Books
Page 125& 126 John M. Gipson.

This Indenture made and entered into April 28th 1849 Sold and confirmed
by me John Harris of the county of Jackson and State of Tennessee to
John H. Carlton of the countya nd State aforesaid Sixty acres of land
for the sum of one hundred dollars in hand paid lying in sd county on
the water of Bear Creek beginning at a Black oak the south East corner
of Absolom Williamd curvey then South seven poles to a stake the Southwest corner of Charles Phillips formily Noah Kuykendall survey thencw
East seventeen poles to a stake the northwest corner of a survey
in the name of Jeremiah Travis thonce south with sd, Travis line one
hundred and nine poles to a Blakk oak & pointers thence west forty
six poles to a hickory on Joseph Pearson line thonce north with sd.
Pearsons line twenty eight poles to a forked chestnur thence west with
sd. Pearsons north boundry line sixty four poles to a chestnyt thence
north Eighty seven poles to a sassafras thenve East one hundred poles
to the Beginning and iIthe said John Harris for myself my heris Executors
and administrators according to the true intent and plain meaning if the
best form o deed of conveyance that one or ever shall be found and forever
defend and forever deSend the said land with all the right liberties
and advantages their unto belonging to the sd. John W. Carlton his heirs
and assigns clear of all claims what soever in witness heerof I set my hand
and seal the day and date above written, signed sealed and delivered in
presence of us Attest Joseph Johnson Absolom Willims, John Harris (seal)

PROPERTY OWNED BY BOB PEARSON HILLHAM ROAD COOKEVILLE TENN.
Sparta March 18th 1855
Mr I pearson Dear Sir: Accordin to my promise when I left you I send
these lines to inform you that I am well & in good spirits my suit in
Court in en-ended & the dession is as follows I get pally & a thousand
dollars in money to be paid to me in four months every thing connected
with suit was all in my favor the sale that they made was made void
Tom witnesses was as good for me as him he did not succeed to his monton
at all, I am now at John Youngs in Sparta I shall be at your house in
a month or two & then I can tell you what has happened since I saw you
last. give my love to all the family Children & all yours & C.
                                        Rebecca Stipes.

        Envelope.

Postmark, Sparta, Tenn

        Joseph Pearson
          White Plains,
(in haste) Putnam Co. Tenn.

ACCOUNT WITH JOSEPH PEARSON THE YEAR 1853 AND 1854 AND 1855

Martin Laycock dct to Joseph Pearson to 80 ppounds of beef $2.50
to 13¼ pounds of bacon   1.35
to 35 pounds of beef   .97¼
to 12 pounds of bacon   1.20
to 2 bushels potatoes   1.00
to 65 pounds of beef   2.07
Received three hundred binds of fodder   9.09
                                                               2.25

Received three hundred binds of fodder   3.00
Received nine Churns at 40 cts per churn   3.60
                                                               8.85

And I paid him one dollar and   .24
fifty cts for the churn   1.50
                                                             $ 1.74

The balance due me Joseph Pearson to thirty pounds and half of bacon.
                                                              33.05
Received 4 churns   4.79
                                                              1.60
Boutum 7 Chares   .87

                                                              2.47

                                                             #2.32

WAR RECORD OF R. G. SMITH.
PROPERTY OF AUSTIN W. SMITH, COOKEVILLE, TENN.

The following is a very limited record of the Confederate Army service of R. G. Smith, written by himself sixty one years after the close of the war and in the eighty- eighth year of his li fe.

When the war between the North and the South came up in 1861, I was twenty two years old, and on May 16th of that year I was sworn into the Army of Tennessee. I had previously enlisted in the first company of volunteers raised in Cannon County, Tennessee, and commanded by Capt. M. R. Rushing. Th There were two other companies raised about the same time, one of which was commanded by H. J. St. John, and the other by Capt. Granville Wood, all of Cannon County.

These companies were sent to Camp Trousdale in Summer County near the Kentucky line and were made a part of the 18th Tennessee Regiment which was organized there. It was composed of ten companies; three from Cannon County, two from Rutherford County, one from Wilson County, one from Cheatham County one from Coffee County, and two others from somewhere up the Cumberland Rive I think.

The first Colonel of the regiment was J. B. Palmer of Murfreesboro., Tennessee. The lieutenant-colonel was a man named Carden who lived in Coffee County and the Major's name was Davis.

There were a number of regiments formed at Camp Trousdale. To the best of ,y recollection they were as follows:the 7ht regiment commanded by ColRobert Hatton, the 8th regiment whose commander I can't recall, the 14thCol. Forbs, the 20th. Col Joel Battle. All were state troops at that time and were place along the northern border of Tennessee on all the mainthorough fares leading into Kentucky, from Cumberland Gap to the Mississippi River.

All the Regiments mentioned were sent to other places except theightteenh which remained at Camp Trousdale until September.About thistime all Tennesse troops were transferred from the state service to theConfederate State's service, Tennessee having seceded from the Union and joined the Confederacy.

We were sent now into Kentucky and occupied Bowling Green. At this place was collected a great army which encamped from September, 1861 to the last of January, 1862. At this latter date, some 8000 troops including the 18th regiment to which I belonged were sent to Fort Donalson. I was left behind on account of sivkness. In fact, I had already received a furlough to go hom in order to recuperate. Just as my time expired, I received the news that th the whole army at Ft. Donalsen had been captured, also that Gen A. S. Johnsen son , commander of the army at Bowling Green , hadremoved to Murfreesboro, Tennessee. At htis place I attached myself tothe 23rd regiment, joining a company made up of my old neighbers and friends, principally whom I had known from childhood. I remained with this company until the end of the war.

Gen. U. S. Grant, who commanded the Federal Army at Ft.Donalson, was now transporting his troops by water up the Tennessee River and landing them at Pittsburg Landing not far from the Mississippi line, and almost in Johnsons rear. This move of Grants caused Johnson to evacuate Tennessee and transfer his army to Corinth, Mississippi. T_his was in March. 1862.

The Captain under whom I was now serving was M. M. Brien, a very prominent young lawyer of Woodbury, Tennessee. He had the best disciplined company that I have ever seen. He was never harsh nor unkind to his men, but he was very positive in his orders and they obeyed him to the lwtter of the law.

WAR RECORD OF R. G. SMITH, (CON)

We now started on the long march to Corinth, Mississippi, from Murfreesboro through Shelbyville and Fayetteville to Huntsville, Alabama. We marched through rain and mud, waded creeks and rivers waist deep. After resting
two days at Huntsville, we boarded a freight train and crossing the Tennessee river at Decatur, mAlabama, we soon reached Corinth, Miss. Here we remained about two weeks. Trains from every direction were coming in every
day loaded with troops, until there was assembled the finest army that I had
ever seen at that time. Here we were wrmed with brand new Endfield rifles
brought from England on a vessel which had run the blockade.

I will digress here to mention the names of several soldiers who like
myself had belonged to Captain Rushing's Company and were not captured at
Ft. Donelson. These men were: J. C. New, John R. Rushing, Becton Carnes, Je
Ham and James Peyron. These, with M. L. Hollis who had lately came from Ak-
kansas and was a first cousin to the writer, were members of Brian's Company. We were in Cleburne's Brigade which was composed of the following
regiments and their commanders: The 2ndTennessee, Col Bate, the 23rd Tennessee, Col. Neal, 24th Tennessee, Col. Wilson, the 35th Tennessee, Col. Hill,
and the 2nd Arkansas, and the 6th Mississippi.

On the third day of April, I think it was, the whole army was sent in mO-
tion headed towards Pittsburg Landing going in divisions on different roads.
When night came we went into camp a few miles from Corinth. An orderwasvread
to us in which Gen Johnston explained his reason for the move. He saidthe
eyes of the whole Confederacy were turned toward us with great expectations.

The next day we marched to within about three miles of the enemy's camp.
Ours was the leading brigade on the road. There was a small company of cavalry in front of us which came in contact with a small troop of Federal cavalry and we could hear the report of the guns. Our regiment quickly formed
across the road and waited for for our little squad of cavalry to fall back
behind our line thus driving the enemy with in reach. There was the pounding
of horses hoofs, then over a rise came our men in fulltil with the Federals
in close persuit. Through our line they came, a Yankee Major and men close
behind. "Fire", came the order and it seemed that every gun answered the. Th
He rolled from his horse in one direction, the animal going in another. This
was the first Yankee soldier, except a few prisoners, that I had ever seen.

We remained at this place all night sleeping on the soggy ground. Wewere
within three miles of Grant's great army. Early in the morning we weremarche
ed out in the direction of his encampment. Our route lead us through adense-
ly wooded country. Soon we heardthe bugles and drums of the enemy. Our brigd
was placed in a suitable position and all troops coming in, were formed in
line with us.

The generals had intended to make the attack that day, which was Saturday
but owing to the rain and mud, many of the troops were miles behind. It took
all that day to get them into position.

As our regiment was first in line, I had the pleasure of seeing all the
army file past and take their places in line-a grand sight. These men came
from the best families in the South-fine blooded specimen, but they had never been under fire and knew nothing of the advantage of position inorder to
protect themselves from under fire. They were to get their first lesson. By
Sunday morning, the great army of Tennessee was in line of battle, fronting
ht a mighty army commanded by Gen. Grant. Orders to go forward were given
early and then the extreme right wing was engaged with the Federals in the
great struggle. Immediately the whole line plunged forward and the two long
lines were gripped in deadly combat.

WAR RECORD OF R. G. SMITH, (CON)

I wish that I had the ability to describe what I saw and heard during this battle. I am unequal to the task and will habe to simply relate a few things concerning the company to whuch I belonged. However, I willsay that bhe booming of a hundred cannon, the screaming and exploding of shells the incessant rattle of musketry, and the hissing of minnie balls made a noise that seemed to threaten universal destruction. If it had been as fatal ast seemed be our unaccustomed ears, there would have been no one left to tell the tale.

We drove the Federal army back about two miles, almost to the river, after an all day fight. We hoped yo capture the whole army but Gen A. S. Johnston waskilled and Gen Beauregard was put in command. He ordered the pursuit_stopped unti morning, althiugh it was known that a Federal army under G n. Buell was marching through from Nashville to re-inforce Grant. It arrived during the night and took position in front of our line, fresh army of 30,000 troops. They proved too strong for our tired soldiers and after another day of hard fighting we had to give up the field and move back to Corinth. Our compamy lost more men in this battle than in any during the whole war. Among those killed was my cousin, M. L. Hollis, who was struck down on the field just as the fighting began. I did not see him fall but saw his dead body as he had fallen.

In the beginning I should have explained that our regiment had but one field officer, the lieutenant-colonel, whose name was Neal. He was act as full colonel andCapt. Brien of our company was appointed, temporiarly lieutenant-colonel. A Capt. Moore was appointed Major. In the first days fight Neal was severely wounded and Moore killed, thus leaving our Capt. to command the regiment through the remainder of the battle. This he did gallantly, but after the retreat to Corinth, bhe became too despondent over the loss of his men that he resigned and left us, although he could have easily been elected colonel of the regiment, Seven of our company were killed outright and twenty wounded, some of them very seriously. We were about sixty strong at the beginning of the battle, so this was a large per cent.

Ashort time after this our regiment was re-organized and our company was consolidated withCapt. Low's company from Rutherford County, Tennessee All our original company officers resigned and left us and we had to elect a new staff. Our Capt. was W. A. Ott, first lieutenant, J. C. New, second lieutenant, J. A. Patrick, third lieutenant, J. M. Witherspoon, orderly sergeant, John Murphy.

The Federal army now advanced to Corinth and formed their line in front of us. Day after day we_expected to engage in battle, but our great surpris after a week or more, G n. Beaureguard with drew his army from Corinth to Tupelo, Miss. about the first of June, 1862. Here we remained untilthe last of July when Gen. Braxton Bragg took command.

Our regiment was made a part of Gen. Bushrod Johnston's brigade. This brigade was composed of the following regiments? the twentythird, the twenty fifth, the sixty third and the fifth Confederate, a regiment of Irishmen. These regiments remained together until the end of the war.

We noe strarted on the long raid inot Kentucky.Our brigade was in General Buckner's division and Gen. Hardee's corp. We were sent by rail to Mobile, Alabama., then on a vessel up the Alabama river to Montgomery, then by rail again to Atlanta, and on to Chattanooga.

I forgot to mention the new officers of our regiment and will have to digress again to name them. Neal, though absent had been made colonel, R. H. Keeble was lieutenant-colonel and Horace Ready, Major. These two last mentioned were Murfreesboro men.

Taking up the description of our line of march again at Chattanooga
where I left off, I continue my story of Braggs raid into Kentucky. From
Chattanooga we crossed the mountain and passed through the town of Spencer
Sparta, and Cookeville, Tenn, thence to Glasgow, Kentucky. From there we
went to Mumfordville where we captured 4,500 Federal prisoners without the
loss ed a man. Marching on toward Louisville, we were suddenly turned toward
Bardstown, Kentucky, and encamping there remained for several weeks. Gen.
Buell was in our rear bringing his army from Nashville. When we turned east
he passed on to Louisville where he was heavily re-inforced. Returned back
and pursued us to Perryville where he made a stand and gave battle. We drove
them from the field and they troubled us no further. Ourcompany lost men in
this fight, among the rest our orderly sergeant. Capt. Ott was seriously
wounded and fell into the hands of the enemy. We turned south and came outh
through Cumberland Gap to Knoxville, Tennessee, where we remained a few day
While here there was an election to fill the place of orderly sergeant and
I was chosen and held the place until the end of the war. This was in October, 1862.

From here we fell back to Chattanooga, then over the mountain again to
Shelbyville and on up to College Grove in Williamson County. I don't remember how long we remained at each of these places, but we were in Murfres
boro by the end of December. When we arrived at this place, we found two
armies drawn up in line of battle facing each other. Gen Rosencrantz, who
now commanded the Federal Army had advanced upon Gen Bragg.

On December 31st, the left wing of the Confederate Army, in which our
brigade was placed, was hurled against the federal right and they were driven back about two miles. The next day there was no regular battle, but
plenty of skirmishing and cannonading . This was Jan. 1, 1863. The next
day our right wing made a desperate assault on their left, but failed to
drive themback. Our commander, Gen. J. C. Breckenridge, reported that he
lost1700 men in short time.

During the night Braggs army fell back to Shelbyville and Tullnhoma. Our
dampany did not lose heavily-only one killed and severalwounded.We camped
at these two places for four months, then moved down around Wartrace and
stayed there until the first of July. Then Rosencrantz advanced from Murfrs
sboro and began pressing us.We held them in check several days and then
started back across the mountains to Chattanooga. We reached there July 10h
and remained until September.

The Federals had followed us , crossed the Tennessee river below Chattanooga and were moving south through Will's Valley to gain the rear of our
army. This move compelled us to fall back toward Dalton Georgia. Here we
were being re-inforced by Gen. Longstreet's corp from the Army of Virginia
we turned west, crossed Chickmauga River and faced the mighty Federal force
on the field of Chickmauga. In the great battle that followed, our comapny
had one man killed and quite a numbrer wounded. Of htese one was numbered
among my best friends, J. J. Davis. Hesuffered a severe wound in the head
and was thought for a time to be killed. He was carried to a hospital where
he soon recovered and came back to us in about two months.

We remained in front of Chattanooga till about the middle of November,
when the division to which our brigade belonged was sent to re-inforce Gen.
Longstreets army in East Tennessee, sent htere to drive the Federals under
Gen. Burnsides out of the state. Burnsides had statted from Knoxville to
re-inforce the Federals at Chattanooga, was met by Longstreet and driven
back to Knoxville, Tennessee.

WAR RECORD OF R. G. SMITH (CON)

Our Tennessee Brigade and Gen. Gracie's Alabama brigade constituted what
was afterwards known as Johnson's Division. Now we bade farewell to the
great army of Tenneassee and started on the terrible East Tennessee cam-
paign right in the beginning of the winter of 1863-64.When we reached Knoxville, Longstreet had Burnside's army surrounded in the city hoping to
starve them out and force them to surrender, but after we left Chattanooga,
Grant attacked Bragg and drove him South to Dalton, Georgia. This gave Lee

Grant a chance to send Gen Sherman with a strong force to relieve Burnsides

As Sherman neared Knoxville, Longstreet undertook to force Burnsides to
surrender by capturing one of his main forts. I think where were three bri-
gades selected to storm Ft. Sanders, our being one of them. The attempt
was made but it was a failure. The Confederate loss was considerable, but
our brigade fortunately suffered but little. The night the siege of Knoxville was raised we passed on into upper East Tennessee. The Federalsfollow
ed at some distance and at a little place called Bean's Station, weturned
upon them and drove them back.This was a considerable fight, butour loss we
not great. I don't know their loss, but they followed us nofurther.This was
some time in December, 1863.

We were moved from place to place, staying some time at Dandrige, then
at Morristown where we remained a month, perhaps. This was one of the cold-
est winters I have wver experienced. The mountains were covered with snow
all the time and in the valleys the ground was frozen so hard that travel-
ing was difficult. We had frequent skirmishes with Yankee Cavalry, but
these did not amount to much.

We reached Bristol about the first of April, 1864, and remained until
May when we were marched to Abingdon, Virginia. At htis place we took cars
and reached Richmond May, 5, 1864. We were a rough, miserable looking set
of men. While in East Tennesseewe were cut off from the outside world, all
railroad bridges having been destroyed. We lived on what we could pick up
    from the surrounding country. We suffered for both food and clothing.
Someof the men wore barefooted. The merchants of Richmons seeing our condition, came with armsful of shoes and gave each needy man a pair. Soon after
this we drew clothing from the War Department and were were fixed up very
well.

At this time Gen Grant was in charge of the Federal army in Virginia,
and he and Gen Lee were making the long desperate struggle above Richmond.
Longstreet's corp had preceded us from East Tennessee and was with Lee's
army. We expected to be sent there, but also instead we were sent down the
James River to Chaffin's Farm on May 6th. We did not know there any Yankees
near us, so went into camp expecting to get agood nights rest, but just
after dark we were aroused by the beating of the long roll and
hurried across the river on a pontoon bridge from the north to the south
side of the river. After crossing, we struck the pike leading from Richmond
to Petersburg and headed toward the latter place. We traveled a few miles
and then camped till morning.When daylight came to our great surprise, we
found ourselves facing a Bederal army. Gen. B. F. Butler had landed on the
south side of the river a few miles from Petersburg and it was this force
that we were now facing. We soon got into a fight with them at a station
on the railriad leading from Petersburg to Richmond called Port Mellthall
Junction.

We were in a shallow cut of the railroad which served us for a breastwork.
Here, when the cannonading was at its worst a shell exploded a few feet
above my head and a fragment cut through the crown of my hat and gashed my
head. I was knocked unconscious and put out of business for three weeks. This
was my first blood that I had shed since I had enlisted. I was sent to the
hospital at Petersburg.

The fighting continued for several days and the wounded were being brought
in every day. The surgeons were kept busy dressing wounds and amputating limb
While I was here our brigade fought a hard battle at Drury's Bluff about half
way between Petersburg and Richmond. The Confederates won in this fight.This
was th only time I was ever absent, when our brigade went into a fight.

I rejoined my company at htis place where we were under continual shell-
fire from gunboats till the fifteenth of June. The shelling did us smalll
damage but was very annoying.

About this time Lee and Grant reached James River about twenty milesbelow
Richmond and G_ant began putting his whole army across. Lee had tomove up the
river several miles to a pontoon bridge in order to cross, sothe front guard
of Grant's army reashed the vicinity of Petersburg two days before Lee arrived with his forces. On the fifteenth we were hurried to the defense of Peters
burg. That day we met the advance guard of Grant's army about six miles east
of town. It was after night and we slept on the ground in line of battle.
The enemy in our immediate front was commanded by Gen Hancock. When we awoke
in the morning we found ourselves in fullview of the enemy . They seemed to
resting quietly and showed no signs of advancing. We went to work cutting
a ditch for our protection.We weren on an elevation upon which stood a dwelling house, known I htink as the Webb House. The position of my company lay
through the garedn belonging to this place. By noon we had our ditch finished
and were prepared for what we knew was coming.About one o'clock there was agn
great commotionamong the enemy. They began forming line to advance and came
marching over the open-space between our lines. About half way came within
range of our guns and every man in our brigade rose at the command and poured
such a deadly volley of musketry and artillery into their ranks that they be-
game panis striken and fell back in confusion leaving the ground strewn with
their slain. They soon rallied and came again with the same results. This
was repeated foyr or times that afternoon and they were driven boak every
time. Night came but the fighting continued all night long.

At the foot of a hill in front of us there was some low ground which they
reached and occupied during the night. This preved to be a heavy forcefor
just at daybreak they rushed upon us in such overwhelming numbers that we
were forced to give up our position and fall back a short distance. In this
awful struggle I lost two of my best freinds, Alf Wimberly and Albert Justice
both of whom were captured and sent to a northern prison. This was June",
17, 1864.

We now took another position still in sight of the enemy. They now massed a
strong force and began to advance toward us, but we were prepared for we
had been re-inforced with another brigade and a battery of artillery. When
they got within range the infantry and artilleryb turned loose such a tremendous volley of rifleballs and grapshot that the enemy again turned and fled in
wild confusion leaving their dead and wounded behind. During the remainder of
the day they contented themselves with throwing shells and skirmishing with
our lines.

When night came again we fell back to our main line of works, and our
regiment occupied the very fort that was afterward blown skyward. The next m
morning, the enemy were at us again with a vengance determined to capture ia
this main line before Gen. Lee could come to our aid. They threw one heavy
force after another against us during the day, but were repulsed each time.
This was June 18th and just as night fell again Gen. Lee's army began to
arrive and take their places in line of battle. When morning dawned everything along that great line was as still as a country Sabbath day. The enemy
knew that htey were again facing the great army of Northern Virginia. The
calm did not last long, but instead of attacking they began shelling us fu-
riously, in fact did not cease for many months for we remained here until
July, 25th. During this time it was currently reported that the enemy were
tunneling under pur position and we expected to be blown to atoms at any time
But, fortunately for us, we were sent from this place to the north isde of
James River about fifteen miles below Richmond. I htink that the troops who
took our place in that fort were from South Carolina.It was only three or
four days after we left that it was blown up and every man in it killed.
While we stayed thereour loss was considerable. Col. Keeble of Murfreesboro,
was killed and also Col. Fulton of Fayetteville. Our company lost only one
man, but several wounded.

There was small force of Federals on the north side of the river and our
lintle brigade was sent to hold them back. I can't describe in detail what
we had to undergo while on this side of the river . We were inder fire nearly all the time from the last of July until November, when we were sent
back to the ditches in front of Petersburg. There were sometiems on one part
of the line then on the other, helping to hold it during the long, cold
winter of 1864-65. The shelling and sharp-shooting went on day and night and
it was easy for us to see that our lines were being gradually depleted with
out hope of being recruited. We knew that Gen. Grant's army was beingre-in-
forced steadily untilhe had all the men he needed. I became convinced during
the winter that our cause was hopeless. On April, 2, 1865, the enemy moved
against our line with an overwhelming force, broke it, and started our
army towards its doom at Appomatox. During htis days great struggle against
such heavy odds, I like several others was forced to surrender. This ended
my career as a fighting soldier. About one hindred men from our brigade were
captured and sent on cars down to City Point at the mouth of James River.
There they were placed aboard a steam vessel and sent up Chesapeake Bay to
Point Lookout, Maryland. This prison was located on a little neck of land wh
where the Potomac Riverenters the bay. We were kept there until June 22. We
were captured on Sunday, April 2, and the next Sunday Gen. Lee surrendered
his army to Gen G a nt with the atipulation that his men were to be paroled
and sent home. We prisoners did not hear of the surrender until Monday morning. We knew that htis ended the war and wondered when we would be reheased
from prison.

On April 15th, when we awoke in the morning, we noticed that all the flag
had been lowered to half-mast. We knew that something very serious had happe
ened,.but could not learn what until the newsboys brought in the papers and
we read of the assasination of President Lincoln.

Our prospects were very gloomy and it seemed, after this, that all the
prison officials tried to take out their spite on us. Rations had been very
meager all the time, but now it seemed that we were to be starved to death
for we suffered the very worst pangs of hinger.Many of the prisoners sicken-
ed and and there were deaths daily.

WAR RECORD OF R. G. SMITH, (CON)

I had been in very good health for the last three years of the war, but hehe in htis foul place my haelth began to fail and if I'd had to remain there all summer I doubt if I could have survived it. The members of my company who were still with me were: M. C. Neely, A. J. Jernihan, Bill McCullough, Catsby Edmonson, and J. A. Mitchell, whose sister I afterwards married. Bill McCullough died before we were released from prison.

About the first of June, the officials began releasing a few men at a tin time and on June 19th they called for the Tennessenas to report at the Provost Marshall's office. We understood and obeyed with alacrity. After being paroled, we were sent out of the main prison to an enclosure where there were no guards. We ramained there that night and till late the next afternoon, when we were told to report to the wharf where we found a steamboat waiting. We boarde tgis vessel and bade farewell to that prison forever. There are many places that I saw during the war that I would like to visit again, but I shall neber wish to see Point Lookout any more while I live.

A whiel after night, the boat statted up the Potomac River. It had on board a regiment of Indiana soldiers who had been discharged from the army and were on their way home. They were very kind tonmm, in fact I have never seen or met a soldier who had faced us in line of battle that was not kind and treated me with respect. We traveled all night and reached Washington City about seven o'clock next morning, Here we had the problem of getting transportation to Nashville, Tenn. I really suspect that we were the toughest lookingspecimens that ever struck the NationalmCapitol. We were directed to a certain place and when we got there we were sent to a second and thent to a third and so on until we finally found the right place and bought our tickets to Nashville.

Late that afternoon we were alloed to board a train and statted home. We traveled through Pennsylvania, Ohio, Indiana and Kentucky. Whenever we stopped on that long journey the citizens treated us with scorn and contempt until we reached Louisville, Kentucky. Then we felt that we had arrived amog our own ppeople. We reached htere before noon and found that we had to wait over until seven o'clock in the maxhing/ evening before we could get a train to Nashville. While we waited the ladies of the citybrought us baskets of provisions and I can tell you we had a picnic. It was the first food we had tated for two years that was fir to eat.

We left Louisville at seven o'clokok in the evening and rolled into Nashville between eight and nine oC8clock next morn ng. There they issued us al tickets to Chattanooga. Med Neely, J. A. M tchell, Jim Colemand and I got of at Murfreesboro and walked home to Woodbury, Tennessee, about twenty miles.

After a rest I went to work to repair the great damages that had been done us by the war. There was not a horse left on myfather's farm and very little of anything else.

Tennessee's government had been re-organized with M. G. Brownlow as Governor. The Legislature had passed a law disfranchising the Confederate soldiers and all sympathizers and enfranchised all the negroes. These negroes and some white scalawags had full control of the state. I was dis-

WAR RECORD OF R. G. SMITH, (CON)

disfranchised about four years. In 1867 the Ku Klux Klan put a quietus on the neger and in 1869 there was a reaction in the state and every man became a voter. From that time for many years the Confederates had control.

I want to relate a little of my family history before I close this story. My grandmother on the maternal side was living during the war and had eleven grandsons to enlist. Only five of them lived through it. One, only was killed in battle. M. L. Hollis at Shiloh. James Hollis and Will Hollis, John Smith, my brother, and Andy Doak died of sickness. Will George was captured at Ft. Donalson and carried to a prison in Illinois. He and a boy named Wilcher escaped and Wilcher got home but Will George was never heard of again. This is a mystery that could not be explained. One Hollis, two Covingtons, tow Doaks and myself lived through.
On my father's side, I had a cousin named Goss, who lost an arm at the battle of Shiloh. I am the only one of them all that is still living.

A large majority of the soldiers of Tennessee were young men unmarried, but they did not remain so long. They were the best in society and genewally married into the finest families of the state. On the twelfth of December I married a)1867, I married a little rosy-cheeked girl named Myra Mitchell and she is still with me. She was twenty two years old at that time and now she is eighty. Nearly all of our old friends have passed away. Of the two companies of soldiers with whom I served I know of only two who are still living.

This writing is a very limited and imperfect record of a soldier in the Confederate Army. Had I written it sixty years ago while everything was fresh in my mind, I think I could have done much better. I want to say in conclusion that with all the hardships and terrible privations that I underwent, I never regretted the course I took. I tried to do my duty to my country to the best of my ability and have no apologies to make

I don't know that this littl e sketch will ever be worth anything to anybody, nut I thought that my descendents might some day like to read it. I have written it at the suggestion of my son, Austin W. Smith. I am sorry that I could not write a better one but I have done the best I could at the late day.

(My father died May, 23, 1929 at the age of 90 years, 4 months and 4 days)

Austin W. Smith.
Austin W. Smith furnished this copy of his fathers war record .
Mr. Smith (Austin W. Smith) was for many years Dean of the Tennessee Polytechnic Instituta, Cookeville, Tenn.

CONFEDERATE VETERAN TELLS OF
EXPERIENCE IN FEDERAL PRISON.
BY R. G. SMITH.

RECORDS OWNED BY AUSTIN W. SMITH, COOKEVILLE, TENN

On April 2, 1865, General Lee's thin line of defense around Petersburg, Va., was broken and many of his men werecaptured by the Federals. I was serving in the 23rd Tennessee regiment and with others of this same regiment, was seized and taken to City Point, near the mouth of the James river. Here we were herded on a steamboat and carried up the Chesapeake Bay to the mouth of the Potomac river. We were landed on the Maryland side and conducted by our guards to a place called Point Lookout prison. This was located on a point of land lying between the river and the bay, and consisted of a ten-foot board fence which enclosed several acres of ground.Tents were spread in regular order within, the only buildingconsisting of a long, ramshackle, frame imbiding hall.

Six men were placed in each tent with blankets and knapsacks for bedding This was spread on the bare, sandy earth, which was our floor.

Once a day, a fourth of a loaf of bread was given to each prisoner at his tent door. At the dining hall, he was allowed to get a tin cup of pork or mutton. These three articles of diet did not vary while we were at this prison. Run-down and half starved as the prisoners were, scurvy set in and a squad of men was kept busy digging graves just outside the enclosure every day. Acres were covered with graves of former prisoners.

Near the top of the high board fence , a plank walk was built, around this paraded the insolent negro troops of a crack New York regiment. Their treatment of the Confederate Prisoners, solely at their mancy, was unbearabl If a light was struck in a tent at night, a bullet came crashing through. No one was allowed to stick his head out at night for any reason.

A sick soldier who was suffering from extreme thirst crept out to a well near his tent. "Halt", came a gruff command from a burly negro. The man pleaded pitifully, explaining that he was almost dying for water."Damm, you" came the answer, "I told you to go back" Instantly a report of a pistol shocked the listeners. The bullet missed its target but killed a sleeping man in a tent near by.

After this, complaints poured in upon the provost-marshall, who was not a bad man, Soon after the negro troops were removed and white soldiers, trid on the battle field, were put on guard. These troops treated us very kindly.

Gradually we were emboldened to approach some of them to ask small favors. One day I noticed a sentinal guarding somesupplies near the fence. I cautiously approached the "dead line" between us, not knowing what reception I would get. "Would you like to but a watch?" I asked guardedly. He answered briskly, "Yes, sir, have you one to sell?" I studied my reply. "I know a fellow who has one to sell". "Go and tell him to come out here and I8ll but his watch he said in a hearty voice. I still fely my way. " I don't know whether he'll come or not, He amy be afraid you'll take his watch from him" I said. "I'm not that kind of a mann," he said decidedly. "I'd rather give give him a watch than take one from him " "Well, I'm the man who owns the watch", I said, and handed it over the "dead line"
He gave it a critical glance and said, This in a $15 watch, but the crystal is broken I'll give you $14 for it "This was far more than I had hoped to get and you may be sure I grabbed those greenbacks.

CONFEDERATE VETERAN TELLS OF EXPERIENCE IN FEDERAL PRISON (CON)

I sold two more watches for my comrades that day at good prices. I'd luckily approached the man who dealt in second-hand watsbhes.

There was a sutler's shop with all minds of supplies in one corner of the enclosure. With greenback money a man could but almost anyhting he needed. That $14 did me more good than any money I have ever owned, as it just about saved my life.

I shall never forget the morning after the assassination of President Lincoln. When we awoke every flag around the enclosure was flying at half m-mast. Our negro guards, who were still there at that time, were more surly and insolent than usual. We crowded around the bulletin board where all in-structions and any news that the authorities wanted us to know were written Any disaster like Lee's durrender was sure to be posted there. This time the bulletin board was bare.Not until the newsboys began crying the black-border ed papers around, did we know what had happened. A good natured wag remarked " Oh, I see why the niggers are so thick around us this morning. We're in mourning";

About the middle of June, A Tennessee soldier, named Scruggs, had a happy thought. This was to send a petition to President Johnson for our re-lease. To the best of my recollection it was very diplomatic and read some-thing like this:

Point Lookout Prison, Md.

To the President of the U.;S:

The signers of this petition are all Tennessesns and have always been friends to you in your numerous campaigns back in th e old state. We know that the war is over, and remembering the leniency that has hitherto characterized your publiclife, we are confident that you will in-tercede for us and have us released from this prison.

Signed

A few days after this was mailed, all the names of the signers appear-ed on thebulletin board with the instructions that we report to the provost-marshall. We lost no time ingetting to his office, as we guessed the reason for the call.Other soldiers had been called previously and sent home. Pro-vost-marshall Grady was a very agreeable man in all our contacts with him. We were required to take the oath of allegiance and then received our parole papers.

The next evening er were placed on another steamboat and carried to Washington City. Her, after some trouble in finding the headquarters for transportation, we finally foundthe place and received our tickets, and boarded the next train out for Nashville, Tenn.

On the way we did not see a friendly face, being cursed and abused at many places, until we reached Louisville, Ky. Here ladies met us with large hamper baskets of provisions and we were royally welvcomed. We were back in Dixie Land.

A WAR TIME DRESS
BY MRS MYRA ANNE SMITH, MOTHER OF AUSTIN WHEELER SMITH.
PROPERTY OF AUSTIN WHEELER SMITH, COOKEVILLE, TENN

Since there are few oldtimers, now living, who had the experience of making a wartime homespun dress, I thought it might be of interest to the younger generation of girls, who but a dress ready to wear, to hear the story of the long, tedious and laborious process by which we war time girls made our year's supply of homespun dresses.

"From the ground up" is a fitting expression, for most of us not Only picked and seedes the cotton, but alsogathered thr bark and berriesn to make our dyes, and dug the shale or slate rock, as we knew it to make the copperas with which to set the color of our dye. This rock was heated in a large oven until soft enough to be pulverized a dn was then ready for use.

When the cotton had been seedes by hand—this was done at nights chiefly it was washed in strong soap suds, squeezes into large cakes, and placed on planks to dry in the sun. An occasional pounding and loosening of the cake hastened the drying and made the lint fluffy and light. Whwn thoroughlty dry, the cotton was carded, withhand cards, into soft, white, downy rolls to be spun on the old spinning wheels, some of which had been in our families for a hundred years.

There were two kinds of thread: the chain, orwarp, which was made hard by double-twisting, and the filling, a soft, loose thread. All of it was wwxx wound into hanks on a machine called a reel, which measured the cuts of one hundred and forty-four threads. Four of these cuts mad a hank ofthread. One hank of filling made a yard of cloth threequarters of a yard in width. All of the thread was boiled after being hanked, to make it soft enough to dye wall.

We cmmld make five colors of non-fading dyes: purple, copperas, green black and purplish gray. A great deal of white thread was used with these colors in weaving the patterns of the cloth.

The purple dye was made by boiling the bark of the sugar maple tree and setting it with copperas. This made a clear bright color, either a light or dark shade, according to the amount of dye used, of course.

To make the copperas dye, we boiled the shale and set the color with a weak solution of lye made by wood ashes in an old time ash hopper.

The green dye was made by boiling hickory bark orpeach tree leaves and using a bit of alum to set the color. But the cloth was first dyed a copperas color and then boiled in the green dye. This made a clear, bright green color.

The black dye, we boiled black sumac berries andused the copperas to make the first color fast. However, the threadwas dyed purple first, and th then dipped inot the sumac mixtyrs. The resulting color was a rather dingy, weak black, but brave enough not to run.

Cedar tops were boiled to make the gray dye, and copperas was used with it. The color produced was a mixture of purple and gray.

After the thread was dyed, the warp was dipped into a cornmeal starch called sizing, which made it smooth and slick, to keep it from fraying in the weaving.

When dyed and sized, the hanks of thread were put on the winding blades and from these wound on to corn cobs, spools, home made, also.

A WAR TIME DRESS (CON)

From these spools the warp was laid on warping bars, a process almost as complicated as the weaving. From these it was removed by looping the knotted meshes of thread on the weaver's arm. Then began the tedious placing of this knotted warp in the loom. After this was finished, the long, weary hours of running the shuttle to and fro to waeve in the filling continued until the web of twenty-five yards was made.

The warp was made up of all different colors, according to the pattern preferred, also t he colors of the filling made the check material.

Seven yards of this heavy cloth was used in a dress with plain, full skirts, blouse waist, and coat sleeves.

We fashioned our own patterns and stitched our dresses by hand with the thread that we also spun and twisted.

Our years supply of clothing consisted of two od these homespun dresses two suits of underwear of whitehomespum, a woolen balmoral petticoat, a knitted scarf andhome made shoes cobbled by the neighborhood shoemaker.

(Mrs. R. G. SMith(nee Myra Anne Mitchell) was a native of Cannon County, Tenn where she lived during the war and thedaughter of Daniel West Mitchell. She was rhe mother of Austin W. Smith, for many years Dean of the Tennessee Polytechnic Instituye atCookevillem, Tenn. It was Dean Smith who furnished this copy.)

LETTER TO MRS. GEORGE ANDERSON TAYLOR FROM DR. AUGUSTINE C. Somervell
RECORDS OWNED BY MRS. BENTON TERRY, COOKEVILLE, TENN.

University of Virgina
Jan 18, 1857.

Dear Sister Fannie:

Your letter of Jan 4th was recieved yesterday togather with
one from cousin Elen & another from young Jimmy You may imagine how much ple
sed I was at the reception of so many niceletters from friends at home and
especial one from elder Saiter when I tell you that I had been in bed with
chills all the past week I was so much perplexed & feeling so much depressed
by the enevating effect of chills that I had the blues quite bad. I have lot
so much time by being sick that I fear that I shall have to with draw my
name from the number of candidated for graduation my first examination will
be in Chemistry int eh month of Feb the 20th of that month it will be the in
termediate examination & I fear my stand in that branch will be bad I have
missed eight or ten lectures or more in that one study this has all been
doneby chills & you may know that my animosity fir them is great they are
very mischievous little varments & If I had it in my power would banish them
from the earth in short order. I should like to have been at home to have en
joyed the mesryn Xmas with the young folks. Elen & Jimmy gave me a detailed
account of the frolics & fun But as it was impossible for me to be there I
am sure glad thatthey enjoyed themselves & hope all that want to marry may
do so.

I am not a marrying man now at all. If cousin Fannie Green likes Mr.
Geo Terry" & he loves her I hope they may do well AMary I understood that
Hodge was out in Tennexpressly to see "Mollie Taylor" & her neggers hurraw
for Hodge he is as independent as a wood sawyer I glory in his spunk as the
oldfellow said when he fell of the Bridge and broke his neck. Old Skutes goe
like hot cakes among College boys. Jobe Williams if he marries Miss Baby wil
be pitied by me certainly. I have read and heard of snow storms but I never
saw one before today, it has been snowing & the wind has been blowing as old
Alobus had become mtcycated & they had all gotten from under his controle &
blowing from every possible direction it has been snowing and the wind has
been blowing for more than 18 hours more rapidly than I ever saw it the snow
isnow more than three feet deep in manyplaces & five in others it has been
so bad all day that it was impossible to see more than twenty yared before
you in any direction Oh the cold; cold; it is bitter cold, I would not be
surprised if it killed all the snakes in the CountryI hope you have had
nothing of this kind in Tennessee it is now nearly eleven o(clock & I have
been sick & it is so cold I will endeavor to finish tomorrow the cars did
not run tiday on account of the snow storm, I was speaking of Dr. Roan to Dr
Davis yesterday & he told me that Dr Roan was fine young man & that he grad-
uated with more honers than any other young man had ever done befo e or
since at this place in 15 years, that was speaking a great deal was'nt it;
Goodnight I will finish To morrow.
                    January 19th.
It is nwo Monday morning & the bell has rang for lecture but it is an
extremely cold & very windy day & as I have recovered from being quite sick,
I deemed it prudent not to venture out today, Therfore Iavail myself of the
present time to finish my epistle tomyou. the snowis banked up to my window
this morning & is drifted 5 or 6 feet deep in mmny places. The boy has not
brught me any breakfast this morning & I assure you that I am quite slank as
to my appetite and oh, how much I should like to have some of the nice break
fast that is brought to your table this morning. Some of your nice sausage

LETTER TO MRS. GEORGE ANDERSON TAYLOR (CON)

or hash and biscuits & coffee howmuch more would I enjoy it Jonny has just
returned from latin lecture & is well the exception of a cough & he sends
his love and says we will write to you in a few days. I recieved two lottes
from Arks last week onr from Cousin Fannie & other from myfriend Billy Smith
who is despertly in love with Miss Fannie & says he loves her to distruction
he has gotten it into his head that I am in love with her & is quite difficult for me to convince him that he is mistaken Your Uncle's family were all
well & were very much disappointed by the relations in Tennessee not paying
them the expected visit Give my love to Cousin George & the childrend Grandma & Uncle Fent & to all the home folks when you see them & tell them we are
w all at present & hopr they are better Write to me soon & believe me to be
your fond attached but absent brother.
                    Augustine C. Somervell
P. S.
        Love to all yhe servants I have not recieved a letter from Eli in
a month but I correspond with one sweet cousin who lives in Warrentown &
I haw from her regular she is wel & is attending school again.
                                            Gus.

RECORDS OWNEDBY MRS. BENTON TERRY, COOKEVILLE, TENN, (CON)

University of Va, 1857
Mar, 2nd

Dear Sister:

Your kind letter of the 9th of Feb. was recieved several days ag
and would have answered long before this But for the fact that I had the mis
fortune to be sick all of last week with chills & was not in then in a stat
of bodily or mental composure which I consider a requisite in order that one
may write with the hope of being some what pleasing to the recipient of his
letter & with more satisfaction to the writer. To day is a genuine March
on or daughter (no sense) I cannot say which it is but one thing I know
that its very windy & disagreeable day indeed & a good fire seems quite a
blessingbeing very cold. Last week we had beautiful weather, it was fine
Spring warm sun all this week, but oh; to day seems to be cold enough to
pay for it all Well Jammie I just stoped writing a few minutes ago & put
my pipe in my tobacco bag & filled it with a portion of that much abused
plantI am now smoking whilst I endeavor to write Lam Tarry has just come in
he has been to the office and says there is nothing for the Somervells Ter
ry told me a day ot two ago that his cousin Mollie Tarry was to be married
to a Capt. Jeffries of Mechlinburg Va soon; Tarry is a very good boy but I
like him very much indeed Mr. Arnell of Tenn (Columbia) Johnney's friend
has just been in & him and myself have had a dispute about the merit of a
book whicg Jonnie has(Whilem Merster) It is a book which was transleted
from the Germans I htink is very interesting book though it does not givea
very enviable character to the German Ladies or at least I should feel vey
sad indeed if americsn Ladies had the character which the orthers give the
Germans perhaps you have read the book. I have been very much entertained
whilst reading the book as it was written by a German Virginan that portey
the characters of the German Ladies correctly he certainly gives them un-
enviable characters.

News of very scarce at the University there is a great deal of talk
about the innorguation of Mr. Buckhanan and a great many of the students
are going to Washington in the morning about 50 left here yesterday & to
day I should have liked to have been in Washington on the 4th myself very
much but fate have decreed otherwise I was very much surprised to learn th
that Uncle Jim had lost his little baby and feel very sorry for him and
Amelia WeldonClaiborn was at my room a night or twomago and told me that
his mother is dead. She died about three weeks ago. he seemed to be quite
grieved to speak of her. I noticed he was wareing crape and ask him if hi
family all were well and he told me concerning his motherBut all mankind
must taste of the bitter cup which fate had mixed" I was no lesssueprisedt
to learn that the Esqr's banished daughter had returned to her Fathers
house, and that all was well and Christianlike I hear that cousin Kate
Somervell of Ark's is to be married soon now that is pleasing Ilike to hear
of the like and hope that she may have a felicitous and deliertaion(deligh
ful) time indeed. It is getting late & I must finish I hope you have fine
weather i n Tennessee this Spring and that there may be elegant crops made
& that the farmers may get 10cts around for cotton Tony has been down to h
the Gymnascum to excersize but found the wind too sharp that there was so
little comfort while out init he has taken a wise conclusion and return to
his room, he is very busyreviewing his mathematics he has an examination on
thw 11th of this month

RECFRDS OWNED BY MRS. BENTON TERRY, COOKEVILLE (CON)

and I have one at the same time inMateroa Medien' Tonight a week ago the
wash Society had a celebration on Washington birthday, addresswas made by
F. K. Harris of Meclinburg it was a very nice affair they employed a band
& had everything went on very nice the young men promenaded about three
hours with

120

RECORDS OWNED BY MRS. BENTON TERRY, COOKEVILLE TENN. (CON)

University of Virginia
Apr 2nd 1857

Dear Sister:

Yours of the 26ult was recd today And I avail myself of the present opportunity of writing to you in response to your much suprised letter we did recieve a letter from you about a week or ten days ago, but as it is always tge case a duty posponed is seldom or ever complyed with us thus your letter was not answered, I promised to be more punctual in the future When ever we recieve letters in conjunction, Jonny waits for yme & I for him & Time for neither of us however I have no objection s to you writing to us in conjunction If you prefer to do your letters will be answered more punctually in future I was quite sorry and very much surprised also today to learn from your letter that Ann Eslenor was unwell I had not heard before that she was atole sick when you see her again present me kindly to her if you please-I was pleased to learn that cousin George yourself & the childra were well & that the farmers aro blessed with a good & Early spring I do hope that htey may all may make large crops of cotton & corn & that cotton may sell for 12½ cts a lb you said that cousin G. & myself had been fishing & had very good crops for Fale I was much surprised tho hear that it is cold in htis region that I magine fish cant live on the waters before July I recieved a letter from Jimy yesterday saying that all were well at home, & that he had found my last dog, I was quite vexed when ma told me that a fellow Hulit had stolen my T. Q, if Hulit had been comentable I htink he would have felt my stick laid on his coput, with some emphase, And Tome Taylor is going to move to Deer Creek, well joy go with him I hope he may do well-The inhabitants of old Tipton are moving to otherparts of the country & some to their long home & everything is changing according to the Laws of nature so materially that it is probable that I will not be at all home when Iget back home again oh how mutable are all things ni this world, if I get the blues very bad this summer you all mist not be surprised if you see me at home I read a letter vfrom Cousin Will yesterday saying that his Parents desired him to return home this summer And that in about 2½ months he would be at home in Tenn, which made me feel a good deal like seeing my Parents and kin too, Therefore if I come home thissummer you all must not reprovome for it. I am very anxious to see you all again-I do not believe there is one particle of News in College a good many of the students have become Worried & some haw gone home & others speak of going shortly. The examination come of in Annatormy today But I did not stand it in account of not being able to review Anatomy with out loosing a good many of the regular lectures on subjects that I wishe dto know more about & which are important I understood from one of my correspondents that cousin George Terry was discarded by Miss Fannie Green whilst in Tenn, I suppose that you have heard that Miss Mary Torry was married last month to Col. Jeffries Uthey have gone south on a bridal tour, I heard some time since that Miss Kate Arks was to be married to Mr. Eaten they have my wishes for their happiness in life may their paths be strew with flowers of all kinds I have received a letter from Eli myself since Xmas, though I have written to her several times during that time, I reckon she is very busy & has not the time to write I intend to conyinue to write to her untillshe writes to me. Tis late & I must close give my best respects to

cousin George & and the children to grandma Uncle Ted & to my other kin give
my love to all at home when you go to pas Love to the Servant , write to me
agan soon & excuse all mistakes in this & in previous & suceeding letters I
remain as ever your brother,

In closed you will fine a ticket to our intermediate celebration ,
Gus A Claiborn Somervell.

LETTER TO MRS. GEORGE ANDERSON TAYLOR, FROM DR. AUGUSTINE C. SOMERVELL
RESORDS OWNED BY MRS. BENTON TERRY, COOKEVILLE, TENN

University of Virgina, Aprile 24, 1857

Dear Sister:

Your last has been read and I have some lisure time to day I have concended to write you a few lines in answer to your grateful letter.

We have had winter weather during the present week, & the mountain tops have been white with snow for three or four days past. I never saw or heard of such weather this month. There has nothing very interesting transpired here for several days, lastSunday there was a tremendous row among the students the cause of which was ; a little Jew shopper on Saturday night shot two students one of whom was wounded severely in the head-But is better recovering. About 300Students assembled in front of his Jew Shop Sunday morning broke open his door & played the mischief with his merchandis & C. After searching for the Jew several hours, he was found under the bed of one of his neighbors he was taken out in the street by the students &b tied to a tree where the vote was taken wheather or not he should be Linched It is my opinion that the little "Isaac Of York" would certainly have met wiht a severe castigation if not with his death, But for the Thuonstrautes of Dr. Maupin & a few sensible students who were not so much exceted The jew was take to jail sitting on a rail where he is now, I believe his trial is tomorrow.

There are some very hearted men University of Virgina, The soght of of an celebration some onewho surely must have been acquainted with a young man of mt state Mr Barr Tenn, whilst Barr was at the public Hall attendin the celabration A man I say who must have been well acquainted with Barr to took the liberty of going into his room & trunk and from thence he carried $35. dollars of Barr's money? And a few days before this took place some rascal shot at W. Claborn from the street whils A, Claiborn was preparing to retire for the night Therefore I say that there are some rascal Villians in College.

I read a ticket to Cousin Mary Caths wedding some time since done up in very recheche stils indeed I hope that she may nevervrepent of her selection & that they may live a long and happy life &A C I read a lett er from Will, day before yesterday he will be at home about the middle of June. I wish you would send me something nice by him when he returns as I will be sure to seehim either inWarrentown or at C. H. N. C. this summer. I do want to see you all at home so much & if I cant see you you must send me something fromhome by Will I shall write to him & intrust him to bear bO me any thing which the old folks at home may burden him with for me, He is a good boy & I know he will take pleasure in obliging me I heard from Eslie last week & through Willies letter she was well & doing well except that he does'nt like to write letters very much One of my cousins promised to exert her influence in persuading her to write to me I expect a letter from her daily. I read a most charming & fasinaying letter two of them this week. one from my cousin Fannie Somervell & the other from my cousin Fannie Gren they both write beautifully, as Jonnie wishes to write on this sheet I must close Give my best love to your oldMan & to the children Kiss them for me & to G. Ma & my kins in general write soon to yourbrother May you ever be happy

Farewell Farewell,
A. C. Somervell.

LETTER TO MRS. GEORGE ANDERSON TAYLOR (CON)

To Mrs. I. F. Taylor, Tennessee

        This young man promised to leave me this whole leaf but while I was out he has written not only all of the paper, but I fear all of the news. I wrote Elylas night I have not recieved a letter from him in several months, was much pleased to hear Sickly- I expect that much of your enjoyment will be destroyed by Wills going home next summer I hope that he will have much pleasure He is one of the greatest boys I ever saw. How is cousin George getting on with his farm? I hope finely The weather has been bad for more than 3 weeks Glad it has moderated and today is very pleasant. A young man here from the Isle of Wight, and who is acquainted with Dr. Peek family recieved a letter from his brother, who is at a Military School not far from his fathers he wrote in fine Spirits and was perfectly well .He loved opened a letter recieved in the same mail from home and learned that after a few hours writing his brother had been accidently shot by a pistol which he had in his pocket while out with some of the other boys and throwing rocks The young man is very lively generally and is the life of our Range his brother was about 15 I don't believe he has more than smiled since he heard of his death. The session is now on faston the wave and the time will soon come for us to layaside our study gowns for awhileI much pleasure ever in the prospect of meeting one of my sisters thissummer and think that will must feel pretty good in looking forward to the meeting of all of his relations in Tennessee. Nevertheless I think that it is much better not to go home than I should hate to leave home again. Give much love to all excuse mistakes &ct. I am well but have several Lectures to prepare.

    Write Soon tomyour affectionate brother,

                John W. Somervell

LETTER TO MRS. GEORGE ANDERSON TAYLOR FROM DR. AUGUSTINE C. SOMERVELL
RECORDS OWNED BY MRS. BENTON TERRY, COOKEVILLE, TENN.

Univ of Virgina
May 30th 1857

Dear Sister:

Your much valued letter was recd several days since having
been quite unwell for the past 4 or five days I hope that you will excuse
my seeming neglect I said that I had been unwell for the past few days But
am much better this evening I have felt extremely Billious & also have suffered with a bad head ache However I took 12 gr calomel last night I feel
much better to night.

As I did not feel entirely well tonight, I did not attend Society,
therefore will improve my time by writing you a few lines in answer to your
before mentioned. The weather has been very pleasant here for two orthree
weeks And every one hascome out in white clothes.

I was much surprised this morning to learn that Prop "Bledso"&
family were all in mourning for Miss Bledsewho died last night no one knew
what was the disease with which she died Her death was certainly very sud-
den & unexpected indeed Please excuse all mistakes I have to entertain company and write during the time.

One of my friends have justinvited me to his room to eat fried chik
en tonight that is good isn't it a great many students have with drawn
from college and gone home & they continue to leave every day. The time will
soon be here for us to depart we will soon be with ourfriends in Hicksford &
Greensville Oh; Have you heard that, Loraster Jane & Dr. George Stark, They
are marries At last I was very glad to hear of it George has been courting
Miss Loe for about10 or 11 years I hope that they may live long and be happy
I read a very nice letter today from Cousin Fannie Somervell sheepoke of the
enjoyment at her sisters wedding Oh; how shecompliments Uncle Dick forbeing
so good to visit themH, H, Mr Leiper & cousin Lou Eaton waited togather And
every one enjoyed them selves finely--Also had a nice letter from Cousin Fannie Green she writes a very nice letter, and I think is one of the most ac-
complished& keenest ladies of my acquaintance I must beg that you write excuse this short & indifferent letteras I do not feel in the moode of writing
to night. If you do not write to us before the middle of June you must direct
your letter to Hicksford where we expect to be the last of June or first of
July.

My love to all the family & kiss all the children for me.
Your brother and ever time friend,

A. C. Somervell

LETTER TO MRS. GEORGE ANDERSON TAYLOR FROM DR. AUHUSTINE SOMERVELL

RECORD OWNED BY MRS. BENTON TERRY, COOKEVILLE, TENN.

Univ of Penn Phila
Feb 27th 1858

Dear Sister!

Your letter of the 9th instanthas been recieved it gave me much
pleasure in communicating that you & your little tribe were all well & hap-
pylong may you live thusI suppose in this time that money matters in Tenn &
are in a much better condition than they have been during the fall and winter InPhila the Banks are paying apesil I believe & business is going on as
well as ever and I am convinced that the people of the North look more to h
their interest inn banks and money mattersgenerally than those of the South
There has been a deep snow here for several weeks, & there is yet remaining
a quantity in the Streets. Manypersons have been enjoying sleigh riding
in abundanseseveral young gentlemen myself among the number procured seats
in a 6cent omnibus sleigh last Saturday evening & rofde out to the girard
College—There were several ladies aboard & we had a very gay time indeed
I have not felt rich enough as yet to hire a single sleigh at $5.00 an
hour 7 ride out any of my lady friends or acquaintenses & do not think I
shall feel so. John as perhaps you have learned was in the City a few
weeks agosnce he saw all of the sights that was to be seen & was very much
pleased I believe I took him to the Italian Opera to hear Mad Legrange &
Domfre Td Trovator was the opera & tis very grand & striching opera. The
house in which they acted is one of the finest in the world Academy of
Music on Broad St(John was verymuch pleased with the buildingsperhaps more
than with the opera & the magnificantly dressed ladies who were present on
the occasion in white silk and satins low necks & short sleeves Whilest I
had on my over coat & was not at all uncomfortably warm Tis indeed surpris-
ing to see how a pretty woman will expose herself in order to exhibit her &
charms—Vanity thy name is Woman You are very sure that I have been disappointed in Love! Not so Oh no, woman has ever flirted with me or ever wil
as long as I am in sane mind I defy the race of woman I do not wish you orn
any one else to think that any lady everflirted with me, for such is not
the sase . I have merely come to the conclusion that loving and addressing
the ladies is not a very profitable business I don't want to marry& therefore I entend to say as many hard things about the sex as they deserve & b
independent I do not say it and best at all But candidly I will say to you
that I never have addressed a woman so far who did notn confess that she
loved me & would marrie me if the trooth must be told frequently thought-
less young men court ladies whom they think at the time that they love. and
after tis too late they repent of having placed themselves in such a positi
ion Yet don't infer from this that I would repent or flirt with a lady
after going so far. No I would never let her know that Iregreated having
courted her. In fact I have no grounds for complaint against any woman.
But have benemsowthaied with love if this is possible.

My first examination will be held next Saturday week on Chemistry The
old mais that I am boarding with have just gor a piano and they worrie me
no little practicians I think of quitting the premesis soon or after the
examinations are over Tis too bearing to listen to her bang till ten o'clok
at night on a piano. Give my bes & respects to cousin George & the children

as well as to Grandma Uncle Bert & Charley to your Brother,
A. C. Somervell

Write soon

RECORDS OWNED BY MRS. BENTON TERRY, COOKEVILLE, TENN.

Cora Arnold   Virgina Records.

Rev. J. J. Somervell & Lady
Compliments
Tuesday, 11, Oct., 6 P. M. 1859
DR. A. C. Somervell   Miss Mary B. Somervell
" North view "

To Mrs. Ann H. Clement & Daughter
Present
To Mr. Wm. Somervell & Lady
& Daughters
The pleasure of your company
is respectfully solicited to meet
Mr. J. W. Williams at a Soiree,
at Sam Taylors Residence on
the evening of the 10th inst
at 7 o'clock.
Tipton Co. Ten June, 1, '52

Wm. Somervell & Lady Compliments
Requesting the pleasure of your Company
on Wednesday Evening, Nov, 17, 1852
at 5 o'clock
Bobby H. Hamier, Tenn

TO CAPT. JOHN W. SOMERVELL A. A. GEN. JACKSON DIVISION.
RECORDS OWNED BY MRS. BENTON TERRY, COOKEVILLE, TENN.

Feb 1864.

My Dear Uncle:

This is the Second letter I ever write, the first was to cousin Bettie Claiborn. I went to grandma's Friday and carried it with me and they thought it was very nice Aunt Mamie recieved two letters lately from Uncle Walter saying that he was well.

Mr McCall lost all of his Soldiers Clothes but Uncle Walters Servant Bill saved his, Some Negroes stole two bales of cotton from Uncle Tom but he found it at A M Archers to whom they had sold it, but he sold it for a high price than he would have gotten here Aunt Kate and Bet are going to Covington to school to morrow and grandma says they must go there two years. Uncle Jimmie says that he is very glad that they are going. I knewall my lessons this morning and am gettingon very well with my studies. Ma was at grandmas yesterday and it rained so Ido not think she went home MissHenrian sends her tobacco bagand says she hopes you accept it as a token of remembrance Uncle Jimmie had a dining on his birthday. Therewere a great many gentlemen there and he enjoyed it very much . Aunt Mary's mules foot was sore and she did not go. I wish you should answer this letter.

from your affectionate neice
Mary H. Taylor

RECORDS OWNED BY MRS. ALTHA VADEN? COOKEVILLE? TENN

This Indenture made the 18th of March 1815 And in the Year of Our Lord one thousand eight hundred and twenty five Between Benjamin J. Blackburn of the county of Jackson and State of Tennessee of the one per part and Samuel Hardester(?) of the County and State aforesaid of The other part Witnesseth that for and in consideration of the sum of one hundred Dollars to him in hand paid Benjamin J. Blackburn hath Bargained and Sold and delivered a tract of Land containing thirty seven and a half acres Lying in Jackson County in the first District on the waters of P Pigeon Roost Creek Beginning at two Black oaks thence South 80 poles to the Black Oaks and Black gum thence East ——— to a Stake thence North 80 poles to the beginning Including Blackburn's Improvement Surveyed the 26th day of November 1813 by James Tousandsend (?) Day of November 1813 by James D S Sd Blackburn doth Bind himself his heirs and executors administrators to warrant and forever defend the Sd tract or parcel of Land whom ever claiming or to claim whereunto I set my hand & seal Wednesday and Date above written.

Benjamin Blackburn (Seal)

His
Reubin Perkins Alfred Hardyler
Mark

PROPRTY OF MRS. ALTHA DENTON VADEN, COOKSVILLE, TENN.

State of Tennessee------No 3967.

To all to whom these presents shall come Greeting, Know Ye, that for and in consideration of twelve and one half cts per acre, on the third day of July 1824 pursuant to the provisions of an Act of General Assembly of said State of Tennessee on the twenty second day of November, one thousand eight hundred and twenty three by No 275 there is granted by the said State of Tennessee unto Patsy Embry, a certain tract or parcel of Land containing one hundred and fourteen and a fourth acres, a certain tract or parcel, by survey bearing date the 6th day of August, 1825 lying in said county on the South fork of Mine lick Creek waters of the Caney Fork and bounded as follows to-wit, Beginning at a white oak on the south west corner of a thirty acre survey belonging to the said Patsy Embry running South by fifty poles to a white oak thence East crossing the creek at a ten poles in all ninety poles to a poplar in John Harris west bimdry line of his 50 acres tract. Thence North with said line one hundred and seventeen poles to a white oak in the South boundry line of John Hensleys 10 acre tract. Thence west with his line fourteen poles to a Sour wood stump, the south west corner of said tract, Tha thence North sixty poles to a black gum the North west corner of said tract .Thence west one hundred and thirty eight poles to a black oak and Chestnut , Thence South one hundred and twenty seven poles to a chestnut. Thence East sixty two poles to the Beginning, including and exceeding the 30 acre tract on which the said Patsy Embry now lives.

With the hereditaments and appurtenances To have and to hold the said tract or parcel with its appurtenances to the said Patsy Embry, and her heirs forever. In witness whereof William Carroll, Govnor of the State of Tennessee, hath hereunto set his hand and caused the Great Seal of the State to be affixed at Nashville on the eleventh day of Sept. in the year of Our Lord one thousand eight hundred and twenty six and of the Independance of the United States the fifty first.

By the Govnor, Wm. Carroll.

Danial Graham, Secretary.

Recorded in the Registers office Westv Tennessee, February, 28, 1827.
Stith Harrison, D. R.

No 3967 Patsy Embrt, 1144 acres, Jackson County.
Patsy Embry is entitled to the within mentioned tract of land.
T. M. McGavock, Register, West Tennessee.

RECORDS OWNED BY MRS. ALTHA VADEN, COOKEVILLE, TENN.

State of Tennessee No 940-
To all to whom these presents shall come Greetings: Know ye that for
and in consideration of the sum of one cent per acre paid into the office
of the Entry Taker of White Countyand entered on the 30th day of January
1827 pursuant to the provisions of an Act of the General Assembly of said
State passed on the 3rd day of December one thousand eight hundred and
twenty five by No 1270 there is G$_r$anted by the siad State of Tennessee unto
Joseph Hunter a certain tract or parcel of Land containing fifty acres by sur
vey bearing date the 20th day of June 1828 lying in said County and on the
Falling Waters oand boundes as follows, Beginning at a stake and pointer the
poles Mast of the South corner of a survey Eight and one half acre made in
the name of Joseph Hunter Running thence south Twenty four poles to a white
walnut Thence West one hundred poles to a Lynn Thence siuth fifty six poles
to the Beginning With hereditaments and appurtenances To have and to hold
the said Trust or parcel of Land with its appurtenances to the said Joseph
Hunter and his heirs forever.
     In witness whereof Sam HoustonGovnor of the State of Tennesseehim
hereunto set his hand and caused the Great Seal of the State to be affixed
at Nashville on the 20th day of September in the Year of Our Lord one
thousand Eight hundred and tewnty eight of the Independance of the United
States the Fifty third
                         By the Govnor
Daniel Graham
          Recorded in my office in Book B. Pages 368-369
                         R. Nelson Register of the Mountain District
No 940
     Joseph Hunter50 acres White County
     Joseph Hunter is entitle to the within described tract of land
                         R. Nelson Register of the Mountain District

     This Indenture made this the Thirteenth day of December in the year of
Our Lord one thousand eight hundred and fifty three by and between James Dodsn
seign of the County of Jackson and the State of Tennessee of the one part and
James Brockof the County and State aforesaid of the county other part witnes
that for and in consideration of the sum of sixty five dollars to me in hand
paid by the 3rdBrock the receipt where of is hwerby acknowledged hath bargain
ed sold and by the presance do bargain sell and deliver unto said Brock one
peace or parcel of landthat he the srd Dodson bought ofAbsolem William Supposed to contain sixty acres he the same orless cituated being and lying in
Sd county of Jackson on the waters of Peigeon Creek Beginning at a stake in h
the West boundryline of a Sd corner between I sd James Brock and James Dodson
Runningthencewith the calls of said deed of conveyance and the condition line
between sd Brock and him the srd Dodson laking one half of the Spring that
the srd Dodson makes use of including the srd sixty acres more or less to haw
and to hold his the srd James Brock his heirs and assigns forever and the srd
Dodson do herrby warrent and forever defend the same from allpersons whatsoevr
from holding claiming or onany wise lawful demanding ant part thereof in wit-
nessI have hereunto set myhand and affixed my seal This day and date above
written signed and sealed and delivered in presence of us
Attest J. P. Deering , Stewenson D Ward

                         James Dodson(Xhis mark)
                                        (SEAL)

RECORDS OWNED BY MRS. ALTHA VADEN, COOKEVILLE, TENN

This I ndenture made this fifteenth day of September in the Year of
Our Lord one Thousand Eight hundred and Thirty six Between James Brown
of the County of Overton and State of Tennessee of the one Part and
George McGhee of the Coynty and State aforesaid of the other part witness
That the said James Brown for and in consideration of the Sum of Three
Hundred and seventy five Dollars in hand paid by the said George Mc-
Gheethe Receipt whereare of in here by acknowledged Hath given granted
Bargained sold delivered in fuaffed(?) Conveyed and confirmed and by
these presents doth give grant Bargain sell alsin in puff(?) convey and
confirm unto the said George McGee his heirs and assigns forever in the
following tact or parcel of Land situated Lying and being in the County
and State aforesaid on the Thense West with a tract originally in the
name of said Murphree and John Ramsey fifty one poles to a hickery and
Dogwood Thence North with Lornes Borne Line to a dogwood thence vest
with said Line passin Bornes and Wm A Savages corner and with Savages line
to a popolar and two white oaks and Beach Pointers Thence Siuth with
Savages Line Passin his and Fowles and Wm Marchbanks corner with said
Fowlers and Marchbanks Line to the Beginning in the whole one hundred
and Fourteen acres to be the same more orless to have and to hold and to
hold the before Reseted Tract Or Perne Sabd with all and singular the
rights and Profits emoluments hereditaments and apperteinances of inand
to the same Belonging or in any wise appertaining to the only purpose use
and behalf of himm the said George McGee his heirs and assogns forever
and the James Brown for himself his heirs Exicuters and Administrators
doth covenant and agree to and with the said George McGee his heirs
Exicuters & C that the before Renyed Land and Bargained Premises we will
warrent and forever Defend against the wright till interst or claims
of all persons or manner of persons
Bever Creek Containing one Hundred and Fourteen and one quarter of Acres
Running as follows to wit , Beginning ata stake and dogwood pointers
the Northern Boundry Line of Josiah Marchbanks tract Tence East with hai
line one hundred and fifty poles to a elm Enock Murphree South West corner of a twenty zere Tract thence north with Murphree line fifty seven
and one half poles to Stake and Buckeyes.
Whatever in Testimony where are he the said James Brown hath hereunto
set his hand and affixed his seal the day and year first above Written
Signed Sealed and Delivered in presents of James Brown (Xhis mark)
State of Tennessee Personally appeared Before me William Gore Clark of th
County Court of said County James Brown the conveyor in a degree of conveyance of George McGee for 113¼ acres of said land in said County with
whom I am personally acquainted and who acknowledged that he dult executed the said delivered for the purposes therein Contained witness my
hand at office on 27thday of Oct 1837
The foregoing is a correct transcript of the office recevered made
on the acknowledged the within and subjoined deed
Attest William Gore Clk
State of Tennessee, I hereby certify that thhis deed and the certificate
hereon are truly Registered in my office inLeger F. Pages twenty seven
and eight In witjess whereof I John Kennedy Registeredfor the County of
Overton in said state have hereunto set my name and privet seal on Public official seal being provitted for this officedone at office on the
eith day of Mar one thousand Eight hundred and thirty nine
John McKenney Reg for Overton Co

PROPERTY OF MRS. ALTHA DENTON VADEN, COOKEVILLE, TENN.

This Indenture made and entered into this twenty first day of Sept in th
the Year of Our Lord, One thousand Eight hundred and thirty eight between
Charles Sperry of the one part and Henry Frasure of the other part both of
htetown of Sparta in the County of White and State of Tennessee—Witnessed
that the said Charles R. Sperry for and in consideration of the sum of one
hundred and two Dollars current money by the said Henry Frasier in hand paid
to the saidCharles R. Sperry the receipt whereof is hereby acknowledged and
thereof acquitted and foreverdischarged that by these presents doth bargains
and convey and confirm unto him the aforesaid Henry Frasier his heirs and
assigns forever, One certain lot or parcel of land containing forty eight
Square perches situated lying and being in the town of Sparta in the County of White and State of Tennessee itbeing part of the lots No 73 and 74
as laid down in th eplan of said town and the same price of ground which was
conveyed on the 12th day of June A. D. 1834 by Madison Fisk & Robert Montgomery to the said Charles R. Sperry and which was conveyed to them on the
13th March, 1829 by the Representatives of Doctor Lawson Noussa Dec. which
is bounded as follows to wit; Beginning at a post standing at the intersection of thelines of Back ally and turn pike street on North sideof said strct
it being the South west corner of lot No 73 andwith the line of said Back
allyrunning twelve poles Northward by the full breadth of Lot No 73 and 74
to the intersection of theline of a crop stand thence with the line of said c
cross Street Eastwardly four poles to a stake thence by a line Southwardly
parelelled with the stakes twelve poles to a stake in the line of Turnpike
streetthence with said line westwardly four poles to the beginning Together
with the appurtenances belonging or in any wise appurtenances to have and to
hold the the above describedlot or parcel of ground or land with its hereditaments and appurtenances to the only proper benefit andbehalf of him the afore
said Henry Ffrasier his heirs or assigns forever And the aforesaid Charles R.
Sperry hereby covenants and agrees to and with the said Henry Frasier the
right title interest claim and demand of in and out to the above described
lot or parcel of land which its appurtenances will warrent and forever defend unto him the saidHenry Frasier his heirs and assigns forever against the
rihjt title interest claim and demand of all manner name and affixed my seal
the day and date above written signed sealed and entered in the presence of

                    N. Owham,& C. R. Sperry (SEAL)
                    A CKD 20, Sept, 1838

State of Tennessee, White County Personally appeared before me, Nicholas
Owham, clerk of White County court, Charles E. Sperry the within named conveyor with whom I am personally acquainted and acknowledged the due execution of the within deed for the purposes therein contained which is recorded
witnessed my hand at office the 20th Sept. 1839.
                    Test N. Owham, Clerk, White County Court.
State of Tennessee, White County, I hereby certify that the within Deed and
above certified was on the 21st May, 1839, Registered in my office in Book
L, Pages 292 and 293.

                    Test N. Owham, Deputy of
                    Je W. Roberts, Register of White County.

DEED
RECORDS OWNED BY MRS. ALTHA VADEN, COOKEVILLE, TENN.

Charles Cook
Robert D Allison
Chairman of County Court

I Charles Cook have this ady bargained and sold and do hereby transfer and convey unton Robert Allison Dallisro chairman of the Putnam County court and his Successors office forever for the consideration of a and for hundred dollars to me in hand paid certain tract or parcel of land in the State of Tenn Putnam County District No 1 containing by estimation forty acres and bounded as follows to wit, Beginning on a black oak and black jack pointer in a conditioned line between said Cooks and George and James Ramsey runningSouth sixty two poles to a Stake and Black oak pointer fufty two poles to a stake and black oak pointer thence West eighty four poles to a stake in the glade thence North twenty eight poles to a stake in the glade thence east twelve poles to three hickorys and Black Jack pointers thence North sixty six and one twelfth poles to a stake and blck Jack pointer then east twenty two poles to a black Jack and pointer in said conditioned line thence South with said line thirty two and one twelfth poles to the beginning to have and to hold unto said Robert D. Allison and his successor in office foerever I do civenant with the said Robert D. Allison that and Lawfully seized of said land have a good right to convey it with that the said unincumbered I do covenant and bind myself my heirs and representatives to covenent and forever defend the title to said Land and every part of to the said Robert D. Allison and his successors in office against the lawful clams of allepforegeingatseedvensthis the 6th day of June 1854

Charles Cook (SEAL)

Exicuted and delivered in the presents of us this day 6th of June 1854
Sign Jihn Terry
Robison Dyer

Stateo fTennessee Personally appeared before me Putnam Co. Russell Moore, Clerk of Putnam Co Court Charles Crook with whom I am personally acquainted and who Acknowledged that he ecsouted the within Deed for the purposes there in contained which is recorded witnessed my Hand at office this day 6th of Junel 1854

Russell Moore (Clk)
Putnam County Cpurt

The foregoing deed was Received for registration August 10th A. D. 1854 at 10 o'clock A. M. and Registered

W. Baker

State of Tennessee, Putnam County, L. M. Scarlet register of Putnam County k hereby certify that the above are foregoing is a true & correct coppy A Deed executed by Charles Crook to Robert D. Allison chairman of the County cpurt of Putnam County and regis tered in Book A. On Page 9-10

by William Baker
M. N. Scarlet (Regs) of Putnam Co

PROPERTY OF MRS. ALTHA DENTON VADEN, (CON)

Thos. J. Poteet is entitled to the within described Tract of Land.

John F. Voss,

Reg. of the Mountain acre rtact.

Recorded in the Registers Office for the Mountain District in Book No 10, pages 669.

John F. Voss,

Reg. of the Mountain District.

Grant No. 11573, Thos. J. Poteet, 145 acres , Putnam County, 20th Dec,1855.

PROPERTY OF MRS. ALTHA DENTO VADEN, COOKEVILLE, TENN.

I, James W. McDaniel have this day bargained and sold and do hereby transfer and convey unto I. W. Crutcher his heirs and assigns forever for and in consideration of forty five dollars to me in hand paid a certain town lot in the town of Cookeville, Tenn and situated in Block No 3 North and lot No 4 of said block in the plan of said town to have and to hold the same to the said I. W. Crutcher his heirs and assigns forever against the lawful claims of all persons whatever. I further covenant with the said I. W. Crutcher that I am lawfully seized of said land have a good right to convey it and that the same same is unincumbered. I further bind myself, my heirs and representatives to warrent and forever defend the title of said land to the said I. W. Crutcher his heirs and assigns forever against the lawful claims of all persons whatever. Given under my hand and seal this 5th day of Dec. 1859

J. W. McDaniel (SEAL)

Test-R. B. McDaniel
C. R. Ford

State of Tennessee, Putnam County, Personally Appeared before me Russell Moore Clerk Of Putnam County Court I am W. McDaniel the with in bargainer with whom I am personally acquainted and who acknowledged thedue execution of the writtendeed of conveyance to be his act and deed for the purposes and things therein contained which to is Recorded Written by hand at office this 5thday of Dec. A. D. 1859.

Russell Moore, Clerk

State of Tennessee, Putnam County, I, Stephen W. Brown Reg. for said County do certify that the written deed of conveyance was filed for Registration on the 6th day of Dec. 1859 & was noted on filation Book A. pages 104 A105 at 4 o'clock P. M. A was Registered on Book D. pages 28.

S. W. Brown, Register.

I. W. McDaniel
To
Deed lot I. W. Crutcher.
State Tax————50
Clerk fee————25
Reg. fee   1.05
Ack. 5th Dec. 1857

We, James McKinny, Robert D. Allison, Joseph Hyder, James W. M. Daniel and W. H. Barnes, commissioners of Putnam County for the consideration of Thirty threeDollars A 75 cts to us in hand paid by Joseph W. Crutcher have this day bargained and sold and do hereby transfer and convey to said Joseph W. Cruth cher his heirs and assigns forever for the consideration above named the fol lowing described Town lots known and designated in the plan of the town of Cookeville, 1st as S. W. Block No 3 Lot No 2 bounded on the south by Spring Street A on the South by South Street, 2 other lots known A designated in the plan of saidtown as lots No 1 A 4 S. W. Block No 3 Bounded on the North by South Street , on the South by by the land of JohnDitty, To have and to hold the above described town lots to the said Joseph W. Crutcher his heirs and assigns forever and we hereby convey A transfer for the said Joseph W. Crutcher hei heirs A assigns A all the right title A claim that the County of Putnam has in and to said Town lots in as full and ample manner as we as commission ers of said county can, or ought to convey not further or otherwise. Witness our hand and seal this 13th day of Aprile 1857.
Ack. by McKinny, W. H. Barnes A J. D. Hyder.

PROPERTY OF MRS. ALTHA DENTON VADEN, (CON)

	Robert D. Allison	(SEAL)
Test	J. D. Hyder	(SEAL)
	J. W. McD niel	(SEAL)
	W. H. Barnes	(SEAL)

Joseph W. Crutcher
    FROM Deed ----3 town lots , Commissioners of P. C.
State Tax----------1.20
Clerk Fee --------- .25
Recorded on page 4 Book of Putnam County, Tenn
                        Russell Moore , Clerk.

Regs. Fee----1.50 Paid
    State of Tennessee, Putnam County, Personally appeared before me, Russell
Moore, Clerk of Putnam County Court, James M. McKinny, Joseph D. Hyder, A
W. H. Barnes Sr. commissioners of Putnam County, the within bargners with
whom I am personally acquainted and who acknowledged the due execution of h
the within deed of conveyance to be their act and deedfor the purposes and
things contained witness myhand at office the 7th day of June,A. D. 1858.
                        Russell Moore, Clerk.

    THE STATE OF TENNESSEE---To all to whom these presents shall come,Greet-
ings:
    Know ye, that by virtue of Entry No 26, made in the office of the Entry
Taker of Putnam County and entered on the 10th day of February 1855 pursuant to the provisions of an Act of the General Assembly of said State paper
on the 9th fay of January, 1830, there is granted by the State of Tennessee
unto Thomas J. Poteet, A certain Tract or Parcel of Land containing One hundred and forty five acres By Survey bearing date the 17th day of Mar. 1855
lying in said county of Putnam , it being five acres less than the location
calls for on the head waters of the little Caney Fork and on the Mountain
Beginning on a sugar tree and sugar tree pointer the North east corner of the
Tract on which the Poteet now lives, Running thence South with said line eigh
ty eight polesto two white oaks another of his corners, Thence West with his
line eighty one poles to a black oak dogwood and black gum, another of his
corners, Thence South with another of his lines thirty poles to a chestnut
. Thence East fourteen poles to a hickory Wilkerson's corner. Thence South
with Wilkerson's line seventy two poles to a corner, Thence South with Wliker
son's line seventy two poles to two dogwoods and maple pointers, Thence East
one hundred and eighty poles to two white oaks and two maple pointers, Thence
North with a line of a survey in the name of Clark eighty six poles to a ches
tnut in Coopers line, Thence west two poles to a black oak and hickory,
Coopers corner, Thence North with Cooper's line forty six poles to a poplar
Coopers corner, Thence west with his line sixty poles to a double dogwood
and Pointers on a bluff of Rocks, Thence Northfirty five degrees west with
Coopers line sixty two poles to the Beginning , including a part of said
Poteets Improvements. With the hereditaments and appurtenences , To have and
to hold the said tract or parcel of Land with its appurtenences to the said
Thomas Poteet and his heirs forever. In witness whereof Andrew Johnson , Gov-
ernor of the State of Tennessee hath set his hand and caused the great
Seal of the State to be affixed at Nashville on the day of the Twentieth of
December, in the Year of Our Lord, One Thousand Eight Hundred and fifty five
and of the Independance of the United States the 80th year,
            By Governor, Andrew Johnson,
                T. N. W. Brown, Secretary.

LETTER TO MALINDA JARED, FROM RODA BYRNE YOUNG.
PROPERTY OF MRS. EFFIE BOYD YOUNG, COOKEVILLE, TENN.

Nauvou, Ill. Jan. 25th, 1845.

Dear Mother:

it is with feeling of no ordinary kind that I take my pen in hand , this Sabbath morning to address you this letter. We are all well at present, and have been ever since we sent the last letter, which was to David Nichols except little Samuel he was very sick a few days with the hives, but he is now harty as ever. All the children or more fleshy yhan ever they were before. I hope this letter will find you all well. we have not heard from you since we received your letter of the 28th of July we want you if you have not written since to write as soon as you get this letter for we want to hear from you very much indeed. Write everything that you think might be interesting to us, yousaid in your last letter that we should render each other all the satisfaction we could bywriting. I am some what at a Loss to know, what would be the most satisfactory to uoi, howeverI will tell you a lit tleleabout Nawvau Mormonism so called . Nawvou is a city of Saints gathered from many parts of the world as the old Prophet said two of a family and one of of a city to do the commandments of God even to build a house to his name, with a few exceptions I believe they are the best people in the world, all is piese and quietness the people are industrious, virtuous and temperate but upon this is the words of St. Paul verified that they live Godly in ChristG shall suffer persecutions for the hand of persecution has been heavily laid on us and now the world it seems is making preperations to put the iron hand of oppression , Still heavier upon us By enventing the most abominable false hoods ever thought of Either by man or devil and publishing them abroad by this influence, the Charter of this city has been taken away, the next attempt may be to take away our lives the mobers in hancock County is still prowling around like so many blood hounds , or like so many hungry wolves howling over the blood of some innodent sheep which they have murdered to gratify their ravenous apetite they cry thieft and robbery, when it is indeed that the grater part of thieft they speak of really does not exist, while on the other hand beegums have been stolen and the gums found by the Mormons house and the honey in th house of a mobasrat and many such like circumstances they do this in order to justify them selves in the eyes of the people, for murdering Joseph andHiram for they know that thay cannot make it appear that the Mormons did it. they gathered up the chips whereon Joseph bled and sent them one to another, hundrecd of milesas a token of triumph, My verySoul shudders at the th ught of the unlimited wickedness Especially when I think how soon the rath of God will be pored down on them. Shurely all manner of eveil is spoken of us falsely for Christ Sake but we know that through much tribulation we must enter into the Kingdom, but in the mists of our afflictions our hearts are made to rejoice, for we put our trust in that God, who is able to light up a smile, in the aspect of Wo, yea, his Spirit is better then the juice of the grape and is a probation preferable to the Smile of Princess, his favor is richer then the f finestgoald and his wisdom transcendeth all humon understanding his power is Surpreme his plans is founded on wisdom, he will perform his work and accomplish his purpose. Man cannot prevent it, principles ofhis kingdom are princ iples of truth and truth is everlasting as him self therefore his Kingdom wil stand and those that abide its laws will come up before him to dwell in his presence, therefore we will adhere to his statutes we will win out in the new everlasting covenant, not counting our lives dear unto us.

Mother, I often ask ,yself this question, Why am I here alone, withou

any of my connection, why do they not come into this work, the ans is suggestd
to my mind they worship God and they think that is all that is required of
them if this is the case I wish to refer you to the 8th Chapter of the Acts
where a man of Ethiopie had been to Jerusalem to worship and was returning,
reading his Bible when Phillip came to him and preached to him and the firt
water they came to, they went down into it and he was baptized, also in the 1š
thbchapter of Act worshiped God yet she gave heed to the Gospel preached by Gdd
though the Lord ppened her heart that she might receive his word. Now if the
Lord has not^opened the eyes of you understanding to see the necesity of his
Church, being organized according to the New Testament pattern I entreat you to
pray that the Lord in the infervency of your Soul, that he wouldopen your
heart to receive thetruth of all that he has designed for our Salvation. Mother
tellme your mind upon tjis subject in the next lwtter. I must begin to come to
a close give my Love to Grandmother Byrne, and Mother Young and to all inquiring friends. I beg to be able to be excused for my bad writing and Spelling for
the children was very noisy and little Samuel was hanging around my lap. I call
the children up around me and asked them what I should tell you about them.
Francis said she wished I would put her in the office with the letter & send
her to Tenn for to see her Grandmother, Now said she if you write that it willt
tickle them. Vivian sends her love to Grany Byrne, Anna & Martha syas send mix
two. We remain as ever,

                              Yours in love untill death,
                              R. B. & A. D. Young.

LETTER TO L. BYRNE, ESQ. FROM BRICE BYRNE & ANN BYRNE.

OWNED BY MRS. EFFIE BOYD YOUNG, COOKEVILLE, TENN.

                                        Crooked Creek, Ark.
                                        June, 8th, 1851.
Dear Brother:
            I embrace the present oppitunity of informing you that we are
at this time in the enjoyment of reasonable health. We have had sickness in
the family and death has visited us. Our Dorsus is no more she departed this
life on the 13th oflast month, at 12, o'clock. She was taken about twenty days
The physician that attended her Termed the disease congestive fever, since her
death but thiught before it was caused from exposure, and had taken cold,he
had notconsidered her case serious .the health of my family has not been very
good for the two last weeks. Mary Ann & L. V. has been unwell, but are up agai
Williams helth is not improving this summer, thereappears to be more sickness
this spring and so far this summer than has been since we have been in Arkansas. The prevailing disease is called congestive fever. By some called winter
fever And has proved fatal in several instances. I have been anxiously looking
for a letter from you in answer to one sent you sometime ago. I hope you will
not neglect writting much longer. I am always anxious to hear from you and
f amily and all the connection. it has been a long time since I have heard
from any of the connection in your section. None of you seem to bother yourself to keep up a corespondance with us. I want you to understand that htese
lines reach you-Malinda and Joseph Jared And will expect a corespondance from
each of you as though I had directed to you seperately. I wrote to your son,
Alex and requested a more frequent corespondance . he answered me ametiately
and said hw was well, he gives me much pleasure in his communication, all was
in goof helth the last news from him.
            Harvest has just commenced here and the prospect is flattering, the
wheat isbetter than I ever saw, if we shoo have a favorable time for saving
there certainly will be more wheat in the country than ever in this country in
any former season, so think all the oldest settlers. There was considerable
wind and some rain passed last night. I fear it has done damage. I have not
heard from any yet. There is an apperance of more rain , the season has been
very dryhere, but last winter and spring the crops of corn and oats look very
well n buy a little backward. The price of corn is 50cts a bushel, wheat will
probably be worth about 50cts,corn crops having been so short last year, bacon
is worth about 8cts per lb. A common cow and calf is worth about $8.00, beef
will be woth about 2cts, coffee is worth from 16 to 20cts. Sugar 10 to 12.
Dry goods a little on decline but dear enough yet. I have no political news
that is very interesting, not being the year of our election. Save that a
member of Congress, the Democrats nominated Johnson for reelection and I pre-
sume he will have no opposition. Please allow your selves time to write me as
soon as convenant give me the helth of the country, the family news without
stint,, Deaths, marriages the commercial political and All interesting news.
I will also inform you before concluding that the families of the son- in-
laws are in reasonable helth as near as could be reasonably be expected.
Miariam has a daughter two months old and Elizabeth a daughter borned the same
eve that Dorcus died. They have named them both for our dear lamented child.
I nowconclude with a hope of good news from you and that these lines when they
reach you may find you all enjoying good helth. Please accept of the Respt.
and well wishes of myself and Ann and all the children to you all.
                        Brice Byrne& Ann Byrne.
Larance & Sarah By me & family
Joseph Jared & family
Malinda B. Jared & family

Crooked Creek Arks
May, 4th. '53

Dear Nephew:

I avail myself of the present opportunity to inform you and your mother that we are all at present in the enjoyment of reasonable health. The conection here are generally well, I hope Providence will bless you All with equal health and prosperity.

I don't know that I have any interesting news to write, Though if I fail to write you might think I would be treating you with infifference or neglect which is far from my intention. I take as much delight in hearing from my friends , particularly my connection as any personliving, You know that there are only three of the old stock left, and I think a more frequent communication would be better proof of our filial feelings toward each other, tho if there has been neglect on the part of the old ones I am glad to see the young ones unwilling to follow the examples and from yourpromise in your letter to me I shall expect letters frequently from you.Your Uncle Lorance boy have written to me frequently and take great pleasure in receiving their communications. I received a letter lately from Alexandria he informed me of his trip to your neighborhood. I was truly glad that him self and family that was with him, enjoyed themselfs with so pleasant a trip, as he states and found al well at home on his return. I am looking by every mail for letters from my young friends, jog their memoriesa little. I wish you to inform your mother a and Uncle Lawrence & your Uncle Joseph Jared that I would like to read a great long letter from either or all of them, give them all the contents of thisconsideration as though it had been directed to them.

You wished me to hive you some information respecting this country rather a describe I am not a good hand to describe tho proceed to tell you something about it would have done so sooner, but thought I would be better prepared after returning from an expected Tour of surveying in different parts of the country, I have been in the upper part of the county two trips surveying the Northern and Western part of the county, in Praitie Town Ship North of this I found a beautiful country, it was aboutthe first of Aprile, the prairie just beginning to make its grass appear, the Land generally lies wellTimber tolerably scarce, and not so very good, consisting of PostOak, black Oaks, blac Jacks and Hickory, the black jack in this country denotes Strong land such as will bring with a favorable season, 50 bus of corn per acre, or from 20 to 25bb wheat, large blackjack groth denote Strongest of land. Water is tolerable plentiful, some verygood springs, and excellent summer rains. I was also on a water course called Osage, a tributary of White River the bottoms there are excellent and lie very well, the hills are also very rich and not very scarce, The timber , Oaks, of every description, Hickory, Hackberry, Lyn, Sugar tree, walnut cherry, box elder & blue and black ash& Shrubbery or undergrowth huge pawpaw, Spin wood & Sumak, range for horses and cattle not so good as in the Prairie or barrens. The I think hogs do very well. Again I was on Kings River another tributary of White River. I surveyed some very good land, some bottom land and some very good barrens generally Oak and hickory timber out from the bottom and shumak and hazel undergrowth, Springs some what scarce, pretty good range this part of the county where I lived on Crooked Creek consists of Prairi barrens and some bottom lands, generally very good timber, tolerable scarce. w water is to be had in Spgs. frequently very good. Some have to dig the well. Water is generally very good thispart of the county, hard to beat in its general aperance, the grass is excellent, Milk cows fill the pails to over flowing

they can get grass plenty with out going out of hearing the soil here is adap
ted to the growth of almost everything I ever knew to grow any where, corn,
wheat, oats, cotton & tobacco, Irish and sweet potatoes, cabbage, onions and
garden vegetables grow better here here than you would suppose, or even con-
jecture in a northern latitude.

        There is a great deal of broken hilly country here some mountains and
ridges and some places very stony and gravelly, but the cleanest country of
mud and stagnated water I ever saw, the streams generally runs swift and are
as clear as crystal. I can't see any local cause for sickness, not withsatnd-
ing last year was very sickly here, and in some parts of the county, typhoid
fever as the physicians (termed it) proved very fatal , now as respects my
opinion concerning the exchange of your country with this I hardly know what
to say though if I were a citizen of Indian Creek or owned no better than
one of the little farms above Uncle Bills old place as it used to be called ,I
certainly would be facing for Arkansas, I suppose it depends on, presumably on
our taste, contentment is said to be the best fortune. I would be glad , how
wise a choice you would make and would be mighty glad to fine you my neighbor with your mother and many other of our friends. We have had a favorable
winter somewhat changeable, very dry and so has the spring been untill now ,
Monday evening and the rain came in torrents and the water rising fast, so
goods and Groceries that are lying on the river below will be up imediately,
theprices of produce and stock are as follows, hogs from 50cts to $1.00, cows
& calf from $10 to $20 , yoke of Oxen $40 to $50 , corn 20 cts per bushel,
wheat 50, flour $2 per hun

        I will here state before concluding, Elizabeth Gillen has a son, call
him name Brice H. Miriam has a daughter, calls it Malinda. I and The Respects
of all my family to you all and all the cousians, also the respects of your
Uncle,

                                Brice Byrne.

LETTER TO MALINDA JARED, FROM M. J. NICHOLS, SOLDIER IN CIVIL WAR
PROPERTY OF MRS. EFFIE BOYD YOUNG, COOKEVILLE, TENN.

Camp Trousdale,
July, 1, 1861.

Dear Grandmother:

        I seat myself beneath the clamors of the drums and bugles
to drop you a epistle full of confabulation it is with gratitude that I am
granted the great privilege of addressing one by dexterity whose integrity
glitters before my imagination as bright as the most precious jewels, you
have ever treated me with great respect and I will ever feel grateful towards you for so excellent works.

        Oh, but that I had mental ability sufficient to paraphrase my sincere
thanks to one so great and kind I perhaps would have been reckless character
if it had not been for the expostulations of my beloved friends who have been
instruments in keeping me from nefarious acts.

        When I look back on my past life and meditate my opportunities of cult-
ure it makes tears run down from my glimmering eyes as they did from Nebuchad-
nezzer in his sorrows but then I have one consolation, that is I am permitted
the glorious privilege of enjoying a bountiful share of good helth. John is h
good helth and is now on drill today is my time to stansguard and I write
your letter during my time to rest there are fifty eight sick in the Hospital
with the measles and many other contageous diseases one man died last Saturday in Numans regiment, and they buried him yesterday in honor of war. I
happened to be over there when they started with him I went to the burying
(dis, 4 Ms) when we got there we found a camp ground surrounded with tombs.
The Funeral was preached by a very able minister, who is the Chaplain of that
regiment, yhe harbor under which the sremon was preached was about 50 yds
from the grave of the warrior and during the sermon I, (being tired) layed
down to sleep and when I awoke I found myself alone, but ran up to the grave-
yard and they were just putting him in the grave, they covered the body
slightly with dirt and then fired twenty four guns over the grave, which
seemed to carry up honor to the God of battle. I would not like to be berried
here if I were to die but would want to be brought home. I am peculiary
anxious to see you all and miss you to visit us When Father & Mother come to
see us, we are all allowed 40 day during the year, and I will spend mine at
home Mrs. West and her daughter are here on a visit they say rain is needed
at Cookeville. I want you all to write soon and tell me all about the Farm
and stock and helth of your commnity. I received your kind letter on Saturday
morning which gave me much satisfaction.

                      With Love Yours Truly
                        M. J. Nichols
                             To
                      Malinda Jared

P. S.

    Father I will respond to your add soon, Write me soon
                And with accuracy,
                Yours Truly,
                      M. J. Nichols
                   (Moses Joseph Nichols)

LETTER TO D. H. NICHOLS, FROM JOHN H. NICHOLS,

OWNED BY MRS. HAYDEN YOUNG, COOKEVILLE? TENN.

Bristol Virginia,
July, 28, 1861.

Dear Father:

I wrote to Mother two ago when we got orders to stop and go back to Mo. I wrote that we were going to stay at that place some days,amediately after I had written we got orders to go on to Virginia we had left the Rail-road, somedistance and had pitched our tent but we took them down amediatelya and proceeded to execute the command We then got on the cars, that have conveyed us to this point where we have to change cars. When we changed the fact was assertained that the trains was not sufficient to take the whole regiment so part of the regiment have gone and our company with one more is left to go on another train.We wil not get off till morning. Father you know that we did'n anticpate faring as well on theRoad as we did at Camp Trousdale, but that was a mistaken idea for we fare better the way we do is we do not have to the fatigue of drilling and we are as wellsupplied with provisions we with at the Camp. In my other letter I told you of the battles which had already been feught, but they are now recruiting for another battle which I am sure will be much more terable than those of which I gave an account but we are 300 miles from the place where the battle is to be fought so I fear it will be fought before we get there. Father Do not mistake me and understand that I want to get in a batt tlefor I never have said that for if this great and solemn crais could possibly be settled without a single battle I would snatch eagerly at the settle-ment, I would lay fast hold with both hands and cling with more than filal affection to that compromise which would save the spilling of the most precious blood that ever flowed in the veins of the American people, but as the divisions and subdivisions of the people in to parties both political and religious has gone into such measure that it must be settles at the point of the bayonet, I as one who loves liberty as one who feels it my duty to help sustain the liberty due us at the expense of the blood of our Fathers, am ready at any moment to carry this thing into effect, and you may never be uneasy about me, butwhen you think of me let these words comfort me , if in battle I am slain I shall die at my post, It is true enough Father that I would be proud to see you all before we go into battle but at the same time that love for our real Southern rites which first prompted me to leave my home and happy fireside , still prompts meto go on in the grand andGlorious cause . Tell Mother that no matter where I go the burning words she spoke to me two days before I started still hum with me in heart and I know that her words were true when she promised me her tenderest sympathies and most humble prayers and Father let me beg of you and Mother to never cease instructing my younger brothers and sisters in the right way for on such an occasion as this your words of instruction arise in their minds as words of comfort, then they as I now do, will thank you for your words of instruction given us in a proper time. I beg too be excused for this advising although my condition enables me to feel the good of pleasant words spoken in time. This makes me feel that it is my duty to do so. You need not write to me without me Stationed at some point. I shall write often, whih will be gladley handled bt you. Farewell, this leaves me well,

From your Son, JohnH. Nichols

To D. H. Nichols

LETTER TO DAVID H. NICHOLS, FROM ROBERT F. JARED.

OWNED BY GRANDAUGHTER, MRS. EFFIE BOYD YOUNG, COOKEVILLE, TENN.

Sparta, Tenn. White County,
Aug, 8, 1861

Dear Cousin:

Your letter came to hand July, 20th, I and Pa was glad to here from you. We are all well at present but Pa he is in very bad helth, he is out at the Mountain now 12 miles from Sparta, he has been there two weeks and he aint coming home till frost, Crops looks very well here at this time, we have not suffered for rain but little there has been more wheat raised here this yearthan has been raised for many years. Wheat is worth 75cts here corn a dollar.

There is canstant talk here about the war, some of the people is scared half to death I aint scared. I never think about it much. I go about my business like I allways did. I hope these few line find you all well so far s I have no more to write at present I will bring my letter to a close, excuse my bad writing, and look over mistakes and as I am in a hurry so no more at present, I remain

Your friend untill death,
R. F. JAred to D. H. Nichols

LETTER TO DAVID H. NICHOLS, FROM M. J. NICHOLS, SOLDIER IN THE CIVIL WAR.

PROPERTY OF MRS. EFFIE BOYD YOUNG, COOKEVILLE? TENN.

Camped Chattanoogia,
Aug, 3, L862.

Dear Father, Mother & Grandmother:

I again avail myself of an oppitunity which I am always glad of
Happy am I to inform you that I have the consoling privilege of sitting beneath the shade of Tennessee Oaks while I endeavor to communicate my friend-
ship to you with quick steps and glad hearts, we putour feet to Tennessee sohl
on the 27thult , all glad to fine enough uninvaded ground to strike camp on,
also to find water pure and cool We find the weather to be much more pleasan
here than in Miss, the weather, water and prople seem so delightful, that
we feel like we have emerged from a land of dispair to a land of felicity, a
great change has taken place among the Tenn troops, they were thought to be
of the bravest species in Virginia, South Carolina and Miss, but since the m
move they all seem to frown with madness and bravery, the thought of the enemy being among our friends and relatives is sufficient to prompt every country loving man to action amediatley, here we are with in one hundred miles
of home, but of fear of being troubled by the cannon envaders of oue State,
we dare not visit home, and friends. They are wiskedly infesting our vicinit
ies destroying privet property and like roaring lions they are traversing
Tennessee, seeking whom they may devour, they even rob poor helpless women
and children of their provisions and leave crying infants, reaching their
weak hands for bread. What is to be done with the murdors of women and children? it recurs to all at once that they should be treated likewise this is
a thing hard for us to endure without vigorously rushing forward and snatch-
ing them from their positions, as an aegle dose her prey. We are expecting to
have Gens Buel and Mitchels supplies out off in a short time, then it will b
that we will leberate Tennessee. After we get them out off from their beef a
andcrackers, they will fail to get backers and we will drive them forward
as a sheperd drives his heard only we will be little rougher than they usu-
ally are, we will generally order them out of our premises and if theynfail
to respond fairly we will slightly put our bayonets to them and push them
Northward untill they strike their own soil, And when they are convinced that
we are getting in good killing plights they surely will get cold in their
cause as some has already gotten, Before we get done with them we will make
them men of consideration and cause them to think seriously on the subject
of war the whole Northern armey consists of poor deluted scoundrels, who
cares for nothing but money and something to eat, Lincoln has made another
call for troops, nut finds them slow to act they have found out the gril-
ling shame by which the hireling were draged in to the field, If he gets them
at all he will ahve to rais their wages, All that we have to do now to achiev
liberty is a general forward movement with sabers in front pointed at the
hearts of thoseGod-forgetting invaders who so much hars us, and who curl the
lips of derision at Southern rebellion, let us be co-workers in this struggle and add golden feathers to our gleaming laurels which we have so vigorously won on goery fields of battle if thevictories we have gained here to-
fore is not sufficient to prove our intentions, the be-holders is hard to
convince, it ought to prove all at once that we will die fighting for freedom,
rather than be conquered by so unworthy Co-horts. independance is a thing
worth working for and we must work with the whole heart and have spirits, if
we accomplish our design and unless consolidated forces , it will take years

to effect peace the thing has to be settled, some way in a short time, or we
will have a debt hanging over us for ages, but the debt is nothing compared
with the object of our design we had rather have a debt hanging over us throu
life , than be brought under the tyranical laws of the North, we will take
death before subjugation, and debt before Northern laws, there cause must be
an unjust one and they can never complete there boasted Determination, which
they so clamorously difused among nations, in the out set, they boasted of
things they cannot stand up to, and are thisday sorry that they bragged so
strenously fo their power and ability A few more good overthrows such as those
at Manassa, Shiloh, and Elkhornand Richmon and manyother points, wil their
line so much, that it will be hard for them to form a line of battle, after we
getour conscriptions in the Field they had better make their wills for they
must surely die or flee from our soil with celerity, they have already been
running from their post at several points which fulfills our passage from the
Scripture, (the gilty flecith when no one persueth)they have no human regard for civility, but go in for a wicked contest entirely and one thing is
certainly true if they do not change their notions they will undoubtedly fall
in to oblivion with out mercy at their down fall we will endeavor to thrive
ande njoy freedom . The Glittering Monuments of Southern liberty is fast
building the day is near at hand for us to reap ourrteward on earth which will
be pure satisfaction through life, and cause has proven to the world, to be
trulyjust, Nations abroad looks on us as soldiers, laboring for pur just de-
serts England and France are expecting us to be successful in the out come,
not long from this day. We will be free from the North and Northern oppression
there is enough at stake to call forht all friends of Liberty to working for
their country and firesides, the soldiers all seem to be on the right side of
the question, while there is some men in the dungeon of unionism, In a few
days we will complete the work in Tenn and free the prople as well as those
portley fellows who could nto muster up courage to take their own part in the
National struggle, Good for Nashville in a short time. Father we are near
enough for you to come to see us by land, and I want to see you so much as
ever I want to see perticularly at this time try to come soon andI think you
will never regret the trip. Stock is in fine demand at present, beef is worth
10per lb, horses are selling very high since the armyyc came in, a drove of b
beef cattle would pay very well if you could get them cheap. Mother I would
love to see you and Grandmother, and all the children but I rather you would
not come to camp for this is no place for women wait a while and we will get a
chance to visit you this leaves us all in good helth and fine spirits give my
best love and respects to all inquiring friends, tell them all to write me
and be sure and write soon, giving the news in general. I am dear Father,
Mother and Grandmother your dutiful son and will ever remain so,
                    M. J. Nichols.
                    (Moses Joseph Nichols)

www.ingramcontent.com/pod-product-compliance
Lightning Source LLC
Chambersburg PA
CBHW080614270326
41928CB00016B/3055